TEN
WAYS TO
PRAY

To Brett —

In gratitude beyond words for your
invitation that I even write this
book in the first place, and for your
belief that I could do it well.

Yours in Christ through Mary,

Carolyn

"Dine at the banquet of Catholic prayer! Carolyn Pirtle serves up rich morsels from scripture, art, the saints, and daily life to nourish your spiritual growth. Flavorful and easy to digest for beginners, busy Church ministers, and yes, for all those who want to begin again."

Fr. Joseph Laramie, S.J.
National director of the Pope's Worldwide Prayer Network
Author of *Abide in the Heart of Christ*

"Carolyn Pirtle proves herself a wise and seasoned guide to Catholic practices of praying in her helpful *Ten Ways to Pray*. While her thoughts on the ten 'ways' she explores are both practical and helpful, her opening chapter introducing Christian prayer is worth the price of the book: a trustworthy and attractive summary of insights into the mystery of prayer. I highly recommend *Ten Ways to Pray* for people at all stages of the Christian journey."

Fr. Jan Michael Joncas
University of St. Thomas
St. Paul, Minnesota

"What a delightful read! Carolyn Pirtle is a great writer and the book is comprehensive and deep yet has a simplicity in its structure that makes it perfect for someone learning how to pray for the first time. It will also capture the imagination of those who are seeking new ways to strengthen their foundation in prayer. Building on the Church's liturgical prayer, Pirtle takes us on a wonderful journey and unpacks prayer through scripture, devotion, beauty, nature, visual art, music, and more."

Julianne Stanz
Director of Parish Life and Evangelization
Diocese of Green Bay

"Prayer becomes practical with Carolyn Pirtle's excellent book, *Ten Ways to Pray: A Catholic Guide for Drawing Closer to God*. From the what to the why to the when of various forms of prayer, Pirtle helps us improve our prayer lives."

Michael St. Pierre
Executive director of the Catholic Campus Ministry Association
Author of *The 5 Habits of Prayerful People*

Praise for the Engaging Catholicism Series

"The Engaging Catholicism series offers clear and engaging presentations of what we Catholics believe and how we practice our faith. These books are written by experts who know how to keep things accessible, yet substantive, and there is nothing fluffy or light about them. They should be in the hand of anyone who simply wants to live their faith more deeply every day or who teaches, pastors, or parents."

Katie Prejean McGrady
Catholic author, speaker, and host of the *Ave Explores* podcast

"The Engaging Catholicism series is a powerful tool to bring the beauty and depth of our Catholic theological tradition to those who need it most. This series will help many to truly engage our Catholic faith."

Most Rev. Andrew Cozzens
Auxiliary Bishop of Saint Paul and Minneapolis

"The work of the McGrath Institute is phenomenal!"

Ximena DeBroeck
Interim executive director of the Department of Evangelization
Director of the Division of Catechetical and Pastoral Formation
Archdiocese of Baltimore

ENGAGING CATHOLICISM

TEN WAYS TO PRAY

A Catholic Guide for
Drawing Closer
to God

Carolyn Pirtle

McGrath Institute for Church Life | University of Notre Dame

Ave Maria Press AVE Notre Dame, Indiana

Nihil Obstat: Reverend Monsignor Michael Heintz, PhD, *Censor Librorum*
Imprimatur: Most Reverend Kevin C. Rhoades, Bishop of Fort Wayne–South Bend
            October 5, 2020

Founded in 1865, Ave Maria Press is a ministry of the United States Province of Holy Cross.

www.avemariapress.com

Paperback: ISBN-13 978-1-64680-057-5

E-book: ISBN-13 978-1-64680-058-2

Cover image © sedmak / iStock / Getty Images Plus.

Cover and text design by Samantha Watson.

Printed and bound in the United States of America.

Library of Congress Cataloging-in-Publication Data
Names: Pirtle, Carolyn A., 1981- author.
Title: Ten ways to pray : a Catholic guide for drawing closer to God /
   Carolyn Pirtle, McGrath Institute for Church Life, University of Notre
   Dame.
Description: Notre Dame, Indiana : Ave Maria Press, 2021. | Series:
   Engaging Catholicism | Includes bibliographical references. | Summary:
   "In this book, Carolyn Pirtle provides readers with intriguing bits of
   history, engaging spiritual and theological commentary, and step-by-step
   guidance for trying ten distinct ways of praying that Catholics have
   utilized across the centuries and around the world"-- Provided by
   publisher.
Identifiers: LCCN 2020045189 | ISBN 9781646800575 (paperback) | ISBN
   9781646800582 (ebook)
Subjects: LCSH: Prayer--Catholic Church.
Classification: LCC BV210.3 .P57 2021 | DDC 248.3/2--dc23
LC record available at https://lccn.loc.gov/2020045189

*To my friends and colleagues
at the McGrath Institute for Church Life,
in gratitude for all they have taught me in word and example
about the life of prayer.*

CONTENTS

SERIES FOREWORD

Doctrine is probably not the first thing that comes to mind when we consider the pastoral work of the Church. We tend to presume that doctrine is abstract, of interest primarily to theologians and clergy whose vocation it is to contemplate lofty questions of belief. On the other hand, we tend to think the pastoral life of the Church is consumed primarily with practical questions such as: How do we pray? How do we pass on faith to the next generation? How do we form Christians to care about the hungry and thirsty? How might our parishes become spaces of lived discipleship? What are the best practices for the formation of Catholic families? Presenting at catechetical conferences in dioceses on a specific point of Catholic theology, faculty and staff of the McGrath Institute for Church Life often hear the question, "So, what's the significance? Give me the practical takeaways."

The separation between doctrine and practice is bad for theologians, pastoral leaders, and Christians looking to grow in holiness. It leads to theologians who no longer see their vocation as connected to the Church. Academic theologians speak a language that the enlightened alone possess. On occasion, they turn their attention to the ordinary beliefs and practices of the faithful, sometimes reacting with amusement or horror that one could be so primitive as to adore the Eucharist or leave flowers before Our Lady of Guadalupe. The proper arena for the theologian to exercise her craft is assumed to be the doctoral seminar, not the parish or the Catholic secondary school.

Likewise, pastoral strategy too often develops apart from the intellectual treasury of the Church. Such strategy is unreflective, not able to critically examine its own assumptions. For example, how we prepare adolescents for Confirmation is a theological and pastoral problem. Without the wisdom of sacramental doctrine, responding to this pastoral need becomes a matter of pragmatic conjecture, unfortunately leading to the variety of both implicit and often impoverished theologies of Confirmation that arose in the twentieth century. Pastoral strategy divorced from the doctrinal richness of the Church can leave catechesis deprived of anything worthwhile to pass on. If one is to be a youth minister, it is not enough to know best practices for accompanying teens through adolescence, since one can accompany someone even off a cliff. Pastoral leaders must also know a good deal about what Catholicism teaches to lead members of Christ's Body to the fullness of human happiness.

The Engaging Catholicism series invites you to see the intrinsic and intimate connection between doctrine and the pastoral life of the Church. Doctrines, after all, are the normative way of handing on the mysteries of our faith. Doctrines make us able to pick up a mystery, carry it around, and hand it to someone else. Doctrines, studied and understood, allow us to know we *are* handing on *this* mystery and not some substitute.

In order to properly hand on the mysteries of our faith, the pastoral leader has to *know a given doctrine contains a mystery*—has to have the doctrine opened up so that receiving it means encountering the mystery it carries. Only then can one be transformed by the doctrine. The problem with religious practice unformed or inadequately formed by doctrine is that it expects an easy and mostly continuous spiritual high, which cannot be sustained if one has sufficient grasp of one's own humanity. We in the McGrath Institute for Church Life have confidence in Christian doctrines as saving truths, bearing mystery from the God who is love. We believe in the importance of these teachings for making us ever more human, and we believe in the urgent need to speak the Church's doctrines into, for, and with those who tend the pastoral life of the Church. We cannot think of any task more important than this. The books of this series represent our best efforts toward this crucial effort.

John C. Cavadini
Director of the McGrath Institute for Church Life at Notre Dame

PREFACE

This book originated in a series of prayer stations designed by Megan Shepherd, program director for Notre Dame Vision, which is a faith formation program within the McGrath Institute for Church Life (McGrath Institute). The stations introduced different forms of prayer from Catholic tradition to undergraduate students serving as the program's mentors-in-faith, helping them discover new ways to explore and grow in their relationship with God. Several years after their development, these stations were also incorporated into the formation offered to graduate-student apprentices in the McGrath Institute's Echo service program. Eventually, they were adapted into an online resource called the *Prayer Enrichment Guidebook*, by Stephen Barany, then–publicity specialist in the McGrath Institute's communications department. Stephen was assisted in the project by several colleagues, including Elizabeth Clarke, Katie Diltz, Ciara Kanczuzewski, Amy North, Tim Pisacich, Megan Shepherd, and me.

The *Prayer Enrichment Guidebook* provided the foundational structure for this book, and I am grateful for the gift of being able to draw upon the work of the brilliant and talented colleagues who contributed to it. I am also thankful to my colleague Brett Robinson and Ave Maria Press executive editor Eileen M. Ponder for the invitation to write this book, to my colleague and dear friend Jessica Keating for her thoughtful feedback throughout the writing process, to my supervisor, colleague, and friend Tim O'Malley for his support and guidance, and to John Cavadini, director of the

McGrath Institute, for forming me in the vision of Church life that lies at the heart of this book.

INTRODUCTION TO CHRISTIAN PRAYER

WHAT IS PRAYER?

In the midst of life's heights and depths, human beings are often impelled by a spontaneous movement of the heart to turn to prayer. We sense in the momentous a presence—something behind the movements of our lives—and we are inspired to raise our minds, hearts, and voices in exultation, or lamentation, or confusion, whatever is prompted by the occasion. The heart's movement toward prayer is, to borrow from philosopher Martin Buber, the movement of the "I" in search of the "Thou." In this mysterious reaching out, prayer is revealed not primarily as an action but more fundamentally as a *relationship*. When we pray, we pray not to some thing, but to *some One*. We seek comfort and wisdom and guidance from an Other, a Thou.

This impulse toward prayer exists in the heart of every human being ever created, whether they consider themselves to be persons of faith or not, because each and every person has been created in the image and likeness of God (see Genesis 1:26). As such, this interior impulse to pray is like a homing device: it is the human creature's inclination toward its Creator God; it is an indication of the foundational truth that St. Augustine articulated in the first book of his *Confessions*: "You have made us for yourself, [O Lord,] and our heart is restless until it rests in you."[1] Prayer is the heart's seeking out of the only One who can give true rest. Prayer is the heart of our relationship with God.

It is important to realize that this is no abstract relationship, because God is no abstract deity. For the Christian, the Thou we seek in the relationship of prayer is the triune God—Father, Son, and Holy Spirit—revealed by Jesus Christ. In the Old Testament, God revealed himself as a personal God by giving his name to Moses, "I AM" (Exodus 3:14). In Christ, God reveals himself as a Trinity of Persons in a dynamic and eternal relationship of love. It is into this divine life that we are baptized as Christians, it is in this divine relationship of love that we are called to participate, and it is through the life of prayer and sacrament that we respond to this call.

Notice our action there: it is through the life of prayer and sacrament that we *respond* to God. Even though we seem to be the ones seeking God—we decide when and where and how we pray, after all—the deeper reality is that our decision to pray is itself a response to the promptings of God's love within our heart. When we experience the urge to pray in life's momentous occasions, or perhaps in the midst of an ordinary day, we are experiencing God calling to us. Thus, the relationship of prayer is *not* actually our initiative at all; it is the initiative of God, our Creator, who made us and redeemed us in love, who invites us to respond to his call and share in the Trinitarian communion of love through lives of prayer and service (as we shall see in our final chapter).

God is a personal God, a Trinity of Persons; therefore, the relationship to which he calls each person is also a *personal* relationship. God calls each and every one of us in the most specific, most particular way imaginable, because God loves each and every person in the depths of their particularity. God is closer to us than we are to ourselves,[2] and in fact, God longs for a relationship with us far more than we long for him. Christ on the Cross showed us this depth of divine longing when he cried out, "I thirst" (John 19:28). The *Catechism of the Catholic Church* interprets this cry from the Cross as an ardent plea from God for the relationship of prayer:

> Jesus thirsts; his asking arises from the depths of God's desire for us. Whether we realize it or not, prayer is the encounter of God's thirst with ours. God thirsts [for us] that we may thirst for him. (*CCC* 2560)

God's thirst for us, God's love for us, is the source of our thirst, our love for him; as St. John wrote, "We love because he first loved us" (1 John 4:19). Implicit in God's love for us is a kind of divine prayer, a longing that we might accept his call to relationship. We pray because God first prays for us. We pray because God first longs for us. We pray because God first loves us.

Prayer is our *response* to God's invitation to communion in a relationship of love, and when we recall that God our Creator is the Source of everything we are and everything we have, we realize that *even our response of prayer is itself a gift from God.* This realization ought to make us aware of our creaturely poverty before our Creator: we are like the young children who want nothing more than to buy their parents a Christmas gift but who must first borrow money from their parents in order to do so. And yet, what parents would refuse to do this for their children? What parents wouldn't love to give their children money in order to see what gift they might choose as a unique and personal expression of love? Prayer is the gift of our heavenly Father, one that God is *always* offering to us, because God takes delight in the manifold expressions of prayer that his children offer him in return for his great love. At the same time, in our poverty, we ourselves can take delight in the way that prayer opens our hearts more and more to receiving the love that God longs to lavish upon us, and we can rejoice in the fact that all we ever have to do to receive God's gift of prayer is show up and accept it.

In this regard, prayer is very simple. Still, this simplicity does not mean that prayer is *easy*. Accepting God's gift of prayer requires a giving over not just of our time but of our very *selves*. In light of this, prayer involves risk. In prayer, we come face-to-face with God, who brings us face-to-face with ourselves and all of our flaws, failings, and deepest wounds. But God does this not to condemn us for our fallenness, but to *heal us from it*. Just as God longs for us more than we long for him, God also longs to heal us from our wounds more than we long to be healed of them. In order to allow God to work within us, to heal us and draw us closer to himself, we have to learn to pray just as we are, not as we imagine ourselves to be, not as we would rather be. This requires us to set aside our egos and humble ourselves before God, who knows us better than we know ourselves (see Psalm 139). There is no possibility of deceiving God in our prayer, only ourselves. But not only does God know us better than we know ourselves; God also *loves* us more than we could ever possibly love ourselves. In prayer, we come to see ourselves as God sees us. We begin to understand ourselves as God desires us to be. And we learn to let go of ourselves in order that God might fulfill in us his desires for us. In the end, the only way we can fully accept God's gift of prayer is on *God's* terms, not our own. But this letting go of ourselves is a liberation from the self. Prayer is how we learn to lose our life in order to find it in Christ (see Matthew 10:39 and 16:25). It involves a dying to self so that God might fill us with a new and more abundant life (see John 10:10).

If we take the passage at the beginning of this introduction from Augustine's *Confessions* seriously, we begin to understand that, ultimately, nothing less than God will ever satisfy the longing in our restless hearts. The logical conclusion from this, then, is that *no relationship in our lives is more important than our relationship with God.* Moreover, there is no standing still in our relationship with God—we are either cultivating it or letting it languish. Of course, the responsibilities of daily life make demands on our time, and there are very real obligations to which we must attend, but if we are not intentionally carving out time for prayer, making it a priority in the way we order our hours and days, then we are neglecting our thirst for God by ignoring his thirst for us. When we experience physical thirst, it is a sign that our body is already dehydrated. When life is going smoothly, we may not be aware of our innate thirst for God, so we may not feel a need to turn to God consistently in prayer; however, if we suddenly find ourselves facing a difficult trial or a severe temptation, we may realize just how dehydrated we have become and how much we need the living water that God has promised to give us (see John 4:10–14). Our relationship with God in prayer is the wellspring of grace that sustains us whether we are experiencing life's heights in a season of feast or its depths in a season of famine; prayer nourishes the soil of our hearts and allows the seeds of love that God has planted there to grow and bear fruit one-hundredfold.

WHAT DO WE PRAY?

As we will see, prayer is expressed in different modes and in different forms, but the content of that expression—the elements of prayer—generally falls into four categories, made easy to remember by the acronym ACTS: adoration, contrition, thanksgiving, and supplication.

Adoration, according to the *Catechism*, is the attitude proper to the creature who recognizes her Creator (see *CCC* 2628). It is a prayer of awe-filled wonder at the sovereignty of God, a prayer in which the heart bends low in homage. Yet, it is also a prayer of rejoicing in the unfathomable goodness of God; thus, alongside adoration, we find prayers of blessing and praise. We bless God for all the gifts of creation he has bestowed on us, and we praise God not just for what he has done for us, but simply because God is God (see *CCC* 2639).

Contrition acknowledges that we have not always been the creatures God called us to be, that we have failed in our relationship with God. If adoration and praise are how we acknowledge God as God, then contrition is how we acknowledge that we are *not* God and seek forgiveness for those times when we have sought to *be* God in our lives. Contrition is the way we ask God to restore us to right relationship with him; it is the necessary first step in the life of prayer (see *CCC* 2631).

Thanksgiving characterizes the posture that should pervade the entire life of the Christian: "In all circumstances give thanks, for this is the will of God for you in Christ Jesus" (1 Thessalonians 5:18). According to the *Catechism*, "every event and need can become an offering of thanksgiving" (*CCC* 2638). *Every* event in our lives—whether pleasant or difficult—is an occasion to give thanks to God, because every event is a reminder that our lives unfold under God's providential care, and that even trying circumstances are mysteriously ordered toward the ultimate good of our salvation. As St. Paul reminds us, "We know that all things work for good for those who love God, who are called according to his purpose" (Romans 8:28). Thus, the entire life of a Christian is meant to be a prayer of thanksgiving, of *eucharistia*, offered in love back to God.

Supplication is the prayer by which we ask God for the things we need. It encompasses both petition, generally understood as prayers we make on our own behalf, and intercession, prayers we offer on behalf of others. Implicit in the true prayer of supplication is not only the trust that God knows what we need before we ask him (see Matthew 6:8) but also, at a deeper level, the faith that God knows better than we do what will be for our greatest good. Often, the majority of time in prayer is spent in supplication; however, one must never neglect to offer prayers of adoration, contrition, and thanksgiving. Otherwise, one's relationship with God will become self-centered and distorted. As we will see, true prayer is about presenting one's needs and even one's self before God in a spirit of surrender; therefore, every true prayer of supplication contains within it the prayer Jesus himself addressed to his heavenly Father: "Not my will but yours be done" (Luke 22:42; see also Matthew 26:39, 42; and Mark 14:36).

HOW DO WE PRAY?

We will explore this question on two levels. One level constitutes a kind of bird's-eye view, focusing on the *modes* in which prayer is expressed; the other delves into the particular *forms* of Christian prayer. Beginning at the macro level, the *Catechism* identifies three modes of expression in the Christian life of prayer: vocal prayer, meditation or meditative prayer, and contemplation or contemplative prayer.

Vocal Prayer

"Through his Word, God speaks to man. By words, mental or vocal, our prayer takes flesh" (*CCC* 2700). For many Christians, vocal prayer forms the heart of their relationship with God, but it is critical that the *heart* never be absent from vocal prayer. In our relationships with others, we are aware when a loved one is participating vocally in a conversation but their mind or their heart is clearly not in it. God is far more aware of such lip service, as Jesus himself indicated through the words of the prophet Isaiah: "This people honors me with their lips, but their hearts are far from me" (Matthew 15:8; see Isaiah 29:13). Jesus calls people who pray in this way "hypocrites" (Matthew 15:7)—people who are acting a part in order to deceive themselves or others, or even God. The humble person is the opposite of the hypocrite, for where the hypocrite presents herself in the most flattering light (think of how most people present themselves on social media), the humble person sees herself truthfully, as God sees her, and allows this truth to be the foundation on which all relationships are built, including the relationship of prayer.

Vocal prayer is the prayer of the poor in spirit; it is the prayer of the person who does not pretend to have words of his own when it comes to addressing God. It is the prayer of the person who receives the words of the Church as gift, finding in them the ability to express his relationship to God better than his own words ever could. Of course, this is not to say that we should never speak to God in our own words—when words of prayer spontaneously arise in our hearts, these, too, are a gift from God, and we should express them. Rather, it is to say that one should not dismiss vocal prayer as inferior to other expressions of prayer. Undoubtedly, we will face moments in our lives when we can find no words of our own to offer God in prayer, and in those moments, we will realize the great gift that vocal prayer offers. Its humble nature offers us a poignant image of God's own humility in speaking to his creatures in words and, above all, in taking on their flesh in his Incarnate Word, Jesus Christ. In expressing our relationship with God in words, we echo his Word.

Meditation or Meditative Prayer

"Meditation [or meditative prayer] is above all a quest. The mind seeks to understand the why and how of the Christian life, in order to adhere and respond to what the Lord is asking" (*CCC* 2705).

Meditative prayer encompasses practices such as lectio divina, where we pray with the scriptures and ask God to reveal his desires for our lives more clearly, as well as the Examen, where we pray through events of our day and search for God's presence and action within them, asking God to help us follow him more faithfully. There are many forms of meditation that are not explicitly Christian because they do not contain the element of prayer, of conversation with God. Christian meditative prayer is unique because its ultimate intent is building and strengthening a person's relationship with God, which then leads to a deeper knowledge of self and a greater sense of one's purpose and calling in the world. Through meditation, the *Catechism* teaches, "we pass from thoughts to reality. To the extent that we are humble and faithful, we discover in meditation the movements that stir the heart and we are able to discern them. It is a question of acting truthfully in order to come into the light: 'Lord, what do you want me to do?'" (*CCC* 2706).

Meditation is not a quest for self-realization or self-actualization. It is a quest for self-emptying, self-forgetting, for the sake of conforming ourselves to Christ and fulfilling God's will for our lives. Meditation helps us to accomplish this quest by engaging our intellect, our memory, and our will—all that makes us human—in order that, through our humanity, God might show us how to live more fully into our baptismal identity as his own beloved children. "Meditation engages thought, imagination, emotion, and desire. This mobilization of faculties is necessary in order to deepen our convictions of faith, prompt the conversion of our heart, and strengthen our will to follow Christ" (*CCC* 2708).

Contemplation or Contemplative Prayer

Because contemplative prayer is the most intimate encounter one can have with God, it often defies description in words. In attempting to teach others about contemplative prayer, mystics like St. Teresa of Ávila (1515–1582) and St. John of the Cross (1542–1591) resorted to poetic rather than theological language in order to convey their experiences. Along these same lines, the *Catechism* offers not so much definitions of contemplative prayer, but descriptions of it, using beautiful imagery that speaks to the heart, beginning with the words of St. Teresa of Ávila herself: "Contemplative prayer in my opinion is nothing else than a close sharing between friends; it means taking time frequently to be alone with him who we know loves us" (*CCC* 2709).[3] The *Catechism* continues:

- "Contemplative prayer is the prayer of the child of God, of the forgiven sinner who agrees to welcome the love by which he is loved and who wants to respond to it by loving even more" (*CCC* 2712).
- "Contemplative prayer is the poor and humble surrender to the loving will of the Father in ever deeper union with his beloved Son" (*CCC* 2712).
- "Contemplative prayer is the simplest expression of the mystery of prayer. It is a *gift*, a grace; it can be accepted only in humility and poverty" (*CCC* 2713).
- "Contemplative prayer is *silence*, the 'symbol of the world to come' or 'silent love'" (*CCC* 2717).
- "Contemplative prayer is a communion of love bearing Life for the multitude, to the extent that it consents to abide in the night of faith" (*CCC* 2719).

Even after reading all of these beautiful descriptions, one may still be asking, "But what *is* contemplative prayer?" A simple way of putting it is to say that contemplative prayer is just *being with God*—keeping God company, resting in God, allowing God's love to permeate to the depths of the soul.

Contemplative prayer is often described as the highest form of personal Christian prayer, but in the modern imagination, with its tendency to rank ideas in a hierarchical value, the word "highest" can create a misperception not only of contemplative prayer itself, but also of vocal and meditative prayer as they relate to contemplative prayer. Categorizing prayer's modes of expression can be helpful insofar as it can lead to a better understanding of how we approach God in a particular form of prayer, but it would be a mistake to think that these modes indicate a sequential progression. With regard to personal prayer, one doesn't "level up"—graduating from vocal to meditative to contemplative prayer. While contemplative prayer, understood properly as the direct experience of union with the Father in Christ through the Spirit, is the deepest form of prayer, the interior posture of contemplation—ardently seeking union with God—can and must permeate vocal and meditative prayer also. When this occurs, the practices of vocal and meditative prayer, in their turn, better prepare and dispose one to receive the grace of God that is offered in contemplative prayer, and even after a contemplative encounter takes place, they remain indispensable to the life of Christian prayer.

It is also important to bear in mind that different forms of prayer may incorporate multiple modes of expression. For example, the Rosary is built up of vocal prayers (which may be prayed audibly or silently), and yet its mysteries invite a meditative dimension through which a contemplative encounter may take place. Lectio divina and centering prayer are primarily meditative in nature, but they may also open up a path to contemplative prayer. What is most important is to remember that *all of these expressions of prayer are gifts from God*, and as such, they all have a place in one's personal prayer life. God meets us in prayer regardless of how we express it, and God

leads us to new depths in our relationship with him through each
of these expressions of prayer.

Having explored the three modes of prayer's expression, we
can now return to the question "How do we pray?" and begin to
answer it at the micro level, the level of form. Because God's love
for each person is unique, God's relationship with each person is
unique; therefore, each person's relationship of prayer with God is
also unique. For the Christian, this unique and personal relationship
of prayer unfolds in the context of the Church, instituted by Christ
himself, with its rich Tradition of prayer and sacrament passed on
and practiced under the guidance of the Holy Spirit by billions of
believers for more than two thousand years. In this book, we will
focus specifically on forms of prayer taught and practiced within the
Roman Catholic Church.

People sometimes struggle with the idea of Tradition in prayer—
even people of deep faith. They perceive it as something restrictive,
something that inhibits their individuality or freedom; however, this
is a mischaracterization. The word "tradition" itself sheds light here:
a tradition is something handed on as a gift. Think of your family's
favorite Thanksgiving or Christmas traditions, shared from one generation to the next. Similarly, Catholic Tradition, which includes the
scriptures, is like prayer, the created world, and life itself: it, too, is
a gift from God, given to the human family and passed on through
generation after generation to help all people grow in a relationship
of love for God and one another.

Tradition functions along the same lines as traffic laws: when
everyone submits to and obeys those rules, people can travel from
place to place in safety and freedom. If everyone were to decide to
make up their own rules of the road, pandemonium would inevitably follow. Similarly, the Church's Tradition allows for a great deal
of freedom within certain parameters, and while this may seem

restrictive on the surface, it can actually help people grow more authentically in their relationship with God. Catholic writer G. K. Chesterton (1874–1936) illustrates this paradox in his classic work *Orthodoxy*:

> We might fancy some children playing on the flat grassy top of some tall island in the sea. So long as there was a wall round the cliff's edge they could fling themselves into every frantic game and make the place the noisiest of nurseries. But the walls were knocked down, leaving the naked peril of the precipice. They did not fall over; but when their friends returned to them they were all huddled in terror in the centre of the island; and their song had ceased.[4]

The Tradition of the Church is the fence that allows the faithful to play fearlessly and joyfully, like little children. Its boundaries are precisely what give freedom. In Chesterton's vision, removing the fence doesn't merely negate the possibility that the children might continue their game; it renders the children paralyzed by the fear that they might fall off the edge of the island. In a similar way, the person who refuses to embrace the Church's traditional forms of prayer not only may find himself or herself unable to flourish but may even be paralyzed from taking one step closer to God. The gift of the Tradition frees Christians from the burden of having to construct the path to God for themselves. The rest of this book will introduce several forms of prayer within the Catholic Christian tradition in the hope that the reader may discover in these forms new (old) ways of growing in their relationship with God.

HOW TO USE THIS BOOK

Each of the ten chapters of this book introduces a form of Christian prayer, offering a brief explanation of what it is, why a person might choose to pray that way, when and where one can practice that form of prayer, and how one might do so. In some cases, one form of prayer offers several possible practices, as in chapter 6, "Praying through Beauty," which explores how one might pray through nature, visual art, and music.

The chapters are arranged in a particular order, which build on the foundation of the Church's liturgical prayer (see chapter 1). There is an inherent sense of growth: the book begins with simpler forms of vocal prayer to encourage the reader to begin praying, then it introduces practices of meditative prayer and contemplative prayer, and it concludes with a chapter on the Works of Mercy as the overflowing of the love of God cultivated through prayer into the love of neighbor expressed through service. The chapter order is not intended to imply a ranking of importance. Instead, it is hoped the reader will find something helpful in each form described, discovering different ways of addressing God at different points in life.

The beauty of Christian prayer is its capaciousness: within the ten methods that will be discussed in this book, there are as many paths of prayer as there are people who pray, because God calls each person individually to a relationship that is unrepeatable. While each form will resonate differently with each reader, the goal of this book is not to offer a one-size-fits-all approach, or a step-by-step progression through various forms of Christian prayer, but to offer many possibilities, many pathways, by which the reader might explore his or her relationship with God.

With this in mind, dear reader, I encourage you wholeheartedly not simply to read this book, but to *pray* about what you are reading. Whether you do so using one of the forms described or simply by conversing with God, ask for the Holy Spirit's guidance as you consider whether or not to take up a certain practice of prayer, and be assured that you will receive this guidance. Remember the promise of Jesus:

> Ask and it will be given to you; seek and you will find; knock and the door will be opened to you. For everyone who asks, receives; and the one who seeks, finds; and to the one who knocks, the door will be opened. (Matthew 7:7–8)

Perhaps you are reading this book because you are curious about the Catholic Church's traditions of prayer; perhaps it is because you feel keenly the words of St. Paul, "We do not know how to pray as we ought" (Romans 8:26). Whatever your reasons, bear in mind how Paul continues his Letter to the Romans:

> The Spirit too comes to the aid of our weakness; for we do not know how to pray as we ought, but the Spirit itself intercedes with inexpressible groanings. And the one who searches hearts knows what is the intention of the Spirit, because it intercedes for the holy ones according to God's will. (Romans 8:26–27)

You are not alone on your journey of prayer. The triune God is present within you at all times, searching your heart, interceding for you, leading you on toward himself. So if you experience a pull within your heart as you read about a certain form of prayer, pay attention to it. That pull may be God's invitation to approach him through that particular form of prayer. Remember: all you have to do is respond to God.

Not only is God with you on your journey (as if that weren't enough!), but you are also accompanied by your brothers and sisters in Christ, the Church. You make your journey with the saints and sinners who have gone before you, and with all who are making their journey now. As you read this book, seek out the company of your fellow Christians. Pray with them. Take the opportunity to try new forms of prayer with them. If you find yourself struggling (and you will undoubtedly struggle at some point or another), talk to a trusted spiritual companion—perhaps your parish priest, or a spiritual director, or a trusted confidante with whom you can speak about matters of faith. Such a person will be able to provide wisdom and guidance, helping you to discern how God might be speaking to you in your life of prayer, and helping you know how to respond.

Above all, remember that prayer is a *practice*—one that prepares us for the day when we will be with God forever in heaven. In that sense, and in the long run, the practice of prayer—understood rightly as a relationship with God that disposes us to receive the gifts of God's grace in fuller and fuller measure—does indeed make us perfect, but that perfection only happens on the other side of eternity. Meanwhile, in this life, it is *perseverance* in practicing prayer that allows us to progress in our journey toward God, toward perfection, toward *communion*. As any musician or athlete can tell you, infrequent practice—or practice without perseverance—isn't really practice at all. Just as you cannot hone skills on the basketball court or at the piano without daily practice, and just as you cannot cultivate a relationship with a friend or family member through sporadic bursts of contact, you cannot show up to prayer every once in a while and expect your relationship with God to grow. You grow in prayer by praying.

At first, such perseverance may come easily; however, you will inevitably experience various temptations and trials in your life of prayer, and you will also likely experience failure of one degree or another. There will be times when your prayer is riddled with distractions. There will be days when you feel too tired to pray, or days when you might be angry with God for something that has happened in your life, and you cannot imagine bringing your anger to God in prayer. There may be times when you feel as if praying is pointless; you may feel unsure about whether or not God is listening, or about whether or not God is even there. The moments when you are tempted to give up on prayer are the moments when perseverance is *the* most essential. Even if the only prayer you can muster is, "God, I really don't feel like praying today," just start there, and keep going. Come to God in prayer exactly as you are, and God will always meet you there, as long as you don't give up. As St. Paul says, "Rejoice in hope, endure in affliction, persevere in prayer" (Romans 12:12).

Another word for perseverance is "fidelity." Its etymological origins are rooted in the Latin word *fidēs*, often translated as "faith." Faith is what keeps us moving forward on whatever pathway of prayer we have chosen. According to renowned theologian and Servant of God Romano Guardini (1885–1968),

> Faith is a prerequisite for prayer. . . . Prayer can only spring from living faith. On the other hand—and this completes the circle—faith can remain alive only when nourished by prayer. . . . Prayer is the most fundamental expression of faith.[5]

In other words, prayer is how we express our faith in God, and it is how we ask God in turn to strengthen our faith. The only way God can do so is if we turn to him consistently, with fidelity, whether we feel like it or not, and whether we sense any response from God or not. Faith cannot be subject to how we feel, nor can fidelity in the life of prayer depend upon how praying *makes* us feel. The life of faithful prayer can sometimes mean raising our hearts and voices to God in the midst of darkness and silence. Yet the grace that comes with such faith, with a total surrender to the will of God, is immeasurable.

At the same time, this call to fidelity in prayer does not imply an unquestioning rigidity, a stubborn adherence to certain practices, even if we sense that God might be calling us to embrace a different form of prayer. Within fidelity, a certain degree of flexibility is required: as our relationship with God grows, our life of prayer may change—the modes of our expression may evolve and deepen and even simplify over time. But if we are attentive to the voice of the Holy Spirit within our hearts, and if we share our impressions with trusted spiritual companions, we can rest in the knowledge that, over time, God will always reveal to us how to draw closer to him in prayer.

1.

PRAYING WITH THE CHURCH IN THE LITURGY

Do this in memory of me.

—Luke 22:19

WHAT IS THIS FORM OF PRAYER?

For the baptized Christian, the life of prayer exists at both the individual and the communal level. Although we pursue ways to cultivate our individual relationship with God through different forms of personal prayer, we never do so apart from our fundamental identity as members of the Body of Christ. Thus, the life of Christian prayer is lived out in the context of the Church, and the liturgy is how the Church prays together. As Romano Guardini affirms in his classic, *The Spirit of the Liturgy*, "The liturgy does not say 'I,' but 'We.' . . . The liturgy is not celebrated by the individual, but by the body of the faithful" (36). In the liturgical celebration—in which the Church gathers in Christ through the grace of the Holy Spirit to worship the Father in spirit and in truth—the individual prays as part of a community that is far greater than the sum of its members. The individual prays as part of the Body of Christ—as part of a profound unity that cannot be understood on human terms, but can only be accepted in faith, hope, and love.

For this reason, the liturgy cannot be something that each Christian creates for himself or herself; it can only be received as gift, and that gift can only be received in humility. When we enter into the liturgical prayer of the Church, we receive from the Church the words and gestures and postures by which we offer our worship to God together. The words may differ from our usual discourse, the gestures and postures may only be used in this particular context, yet this is all for the greater purpose of conforming us to the mystery we celebrate. And the mystery we celebrate is the Paschal Mystery of Christ: his life, Death, Resurrection, and Ascension, offered to the Father in love for the life of the world, and made present now by the power of the Holy Spirit.

In the liturgy, we participate in the saving work of Jesus Christ, and by the graces we receive in that participation, we are empowered to continue Christ's work of building up the kingdom of God in our daily lives. We are caught up in the divine life and love of the Father, the Son, and the Holy Spirit. We are united in Christ with our Christian brothers and sisters throughout the world and even across time, including all who have gone before us marked with the sign of faith, the angels, and the saints. In the liturgy, we experience on earth a foretaste of the eternal wedding feast of heaven. For this reason, the Second Vatican Council teaches that "the liturgy is the summit toward which the activity of the Church is directed; it is also the source [font] from which all her power flows" (*Sacrosanctum Concilium*, 10). In the end, the ultimate purpose of all of our personal prayer, whatever form it may take, is to help us enter more and more fully into the liturgical celebration, to drink more and more deeply from this wellspring of salvation. Personal prayer cannot flourish apart from liturgical prayer. Our personal practices of prayer must be rooted in consistent participation in the liturgical life of the Church; otherwise, they will be like a blossom that has been plucked from its root. They may last for a little while, but eventually, they will wither away. *There is no form of prayer in the Christian life more important than liturgical prayer.*

WHY MIGHT A PERSON PRAY THIS WAY?

Some Christians struggle with the liturgy. Many, in fact. On one level, this struggle is understandable. The celebration of Sunday Mass in one's parish may include a hundred different distractions that one would never have to deal with in one's own private prayer, such as having to wrangle an uncooperative toddler, sing a least-favorite hymn led by a well-intentioned but mediocre cantor, listen to an uninspiring homily, or extend the Sign of Peace to the person who stole your spot in the parking lot. It may also include prayers with complicated structure and syntax, words that sound strange to a modern ear, or scripture passages that are challenging to understand or accept. Such difficulties may tempt Christians to ask why they cannot simply pray at home or out in the beauty of nature on a Sunday. This question reveals a deeper issue. The surface struggles many Christians face around the liturgy and its prayers, readings, postures, gestures, and even settings are in reality manifestations of a deeper, perhaps unnamed desire to pray *only* in the way one wishes to pray—to exert control over one's spiritual life and, by extension, over God. However, the liturgy invites, even demands, a letting go of any desire for control. Its objective realities (the givenness of its prayers, its readings, its feasts and seasons, etc.) insist and necessitate that the faithful conform themselves to the liturgy, not the other way around. This is indeed a challenge, especially in a culture that prizes independence and autonomy above all things. But for those who are able to set aside their individual preferences and enter humbly into the prayer of the Church, even if it is celebrated less-than-beautifully in its externals, the liturgy becomes God's greatest gift on the pilgrim journey of faith, because it imparts to the faithful God's very life through grace.

This primacy of the liturgy is affirmed in the *Catechism*, which teaches that "in the liturgy, all Christian prayer finds its source and goal" (*CCC* 1073). This means that the liturgy is not one pathway of prayer among several, another option to be chosen as an expression of personal prayer; rather, *liturgical prayer is the bedrock of every path of personal prayer*. Without the graces of the liturgical life, no matter how many hours we may spend in private prayer each day, our relationship with God will ultimately languish, because we have neglected to nourish our relationship with him at its source. In reality, our entire life of prayer should flow forth from and lead back to our participation in the liturgy, for it is there that we are fed by the hand of the Lord himself, nourished as branches of the True Vine. In the liturgy, we offer prayer "not just for ourselves and all who are dear to us" (see Eucharistic Prayer I), but for those who suffer, those who persecute us, those who do not believe. In the liturgy, we learn to see all of creation and our brothers and sisters not as objects to be exploited but as gifts from God to be received in reverence and offered back in thanksgiving (*eucharistia*). In the liturgy, we live most fully into our identity as sons and daughters of God, for in it we participate in the prayer of Christ himself: "Through him, with him, in him, in the unity of the Holy Spirit, all glory and honor is yours, almighty Father, for ever and ever. Amen."

WHEN AND WHERE CAN ONE PRACTICE THIS FORM OF PRAYER?

While most Christians immediately think of the Mass when they hear the word "liturgy," the eucharistic celebration is not the only form of liturgical prayer in the life of the Church. The other sacraments, too, constitute liturgical prayer, as well as the Liturgy of the Hours, a rich form of prayer in which certain psalms and readings designated by the Church are prayed at certain times throughout the day. Given that the sacramental forms of liturgical prayer require a priest (or a deacon in some cases), one can only participate in them either according to schedules set forth by parishes or dioceses or by appointment, and, in general, the sacramental forms of liturgical prayer are celebrated in a church or chapel, although there are exceptions to this (for example, a patient receiving the Anointing of the Sick in the hospital).

The restrictions around the sacramental forms of liturgical prayer do not apply to the Liturgy of the Hours, however, which makes it a beautiful way for lay men and women to participate in liturgical prayer in their daily lives. The Liturgy of the Hours (often referred to simply as "the Hours" or "the Divine Office") developed centuries ago in monastic communities. Today, it is still prayed by clergy and religious, as well as many laypeople. The Hours can be prayed by either communities or individuals, and it can be offered anywhere, whether in a chapel or church, a home, an office, or even an airplane. Because this prayer is liturgical, even if one prays it as an individual, one is never praying alone—he or she is united by the grace of the Holy Spirit to other members of the Body of Christ who are also praying a particular Hour at a particular time. In the Liturgy of the Hours, the prayer is still "we" and not "I"; thus, it is a powerful prayer of solidarity that can be offered on others' behalf.

Scripture forms the heart of the Liturgy of the Hours, especially the book of Psalms, which is often called the prayer book or hymn book of the Church (since the psalms are meant to be sung). As the *Catechism* affirms, "Prayed by Christ and fulfilled in him, the Psalms remain essential to the prayer of the Church" (*CCC* 2586). In these poetic prayers, which are "inseparably personal and communal" (*CCC* 2586), the entire breadth of the human experience is represented: joy, sorrow, frustration, fear, hope, longing, confusion—nothing is omitted. When we cannot find a way to express to God what we are going through, no matter what we are going through, the psalms give us words to pray, both for ourselves and for others. The more we pray the Liturgy of the Hours, the more we are steeped in the language of scripture, and the more we learn to receive and respond to the events of our lives through the words inspired by God and prayed by God himself in Christ.

The Liturgy of the Hours consists of specific times for prayer throughout the day; through it, the Church "prays without ceasing" (1 Thessalonians 5:17). Each time for prayer is known as an Hour, but this simply refers to the name "Liturgy of the Hours"—it does not indicate the length of time required to pray it! Each Hour of the Divine Office really only takes ten to twenty minutes, depending on which Hour is being prayed. There are five Hours in the Divine Office: Morning Prayer, Daytime Prayer (three options, which can be prayed at Midmorning, Midday, or Midafternoon), Evening Prayer, and Night Prayer, along with the Office of Readings, which can be prayed at any time. Clergy and religious commit to praying all five Hours daily, while many laypeople choose from Morning, Evening, or Night Prayer, praying the Hour or Hours most feasible for their schedules.

HOW DOES ONE PRAY THIS WAY IN PRACTICE?

All liturgical prayer utilizes specific texts and books prepared and promulgated by those in highest authority in the Church. For example, the *Roman Missal* and the *Lectionary* contain the prayers and readings used in the Mass, and there are similar ritual books for the other sacraments. The texts and prayers for the Liturgy of the Hours have also been prepared and provided by the Vatican, and these texts *must* be used in this form of prayer. The full *Liturgy of the Hours* (all five Hours for every day of the liturgical year) is available in four volumes, but for the layperson looking for an introduction, a single volume titled *Christian Prayer* contains Morning, Evening, and Night Prayer for the whole liturgical year, and an abbreviated version entitled *Shorter Christian Prayer* contains those same Hours, but includes only one week's worth of prayers for seasons such as Advent or Lent, and only certain major feast days. There are also a number of apps available that offer the Liturgy of the Hours. These are especially helpful for those who travel or commute, and they can also be useful learning tools, but it is well worth using the actual books to pray rather than looking at a screen.

That said, it can be difficult to learn to pray the Liturgy of the Hours on one's own; the best way to do so is from someone who knows it well. If you are new to the Hours, consider asking a priest at your parish to help you learn the prayers and navigate the book(s). This process in itself can be a gift: we receive the faith from others, and we learn to pray from others as well. Asking someone to help you learn a new form of prayer is a profound way to grow in relationship with that person, for, as Jesus promised, "Where two or three are gathered together in my name, there am I in the midst of them" (Matthew 18:20).

In discerning whether or not to incorporate the Liturgy of the Hours into your prayer life, start by making an honest assessment of your current schedule. Perhaps at the moment you are truly unable to pray Morning or Evening Prayer. Or perhaps God is inviting you to create room in your day for prayer by letting go of habits or practices that are less worthy of your time. If you are unsure of where to start, Night Prayer is by far the shortest of the Hours; it can be prayed in five to ten minutes just before going to sleep and is a wonderful gateway to this rich form of prayer, through which you can consecrate the hours of your day to God and join your prayer to those of your brothers and sisters in Christ throughout the world.

2.

PRAYING WITH DEVOTIONS

I will praise you, LORD, with all my heart;
    I will declare all your wondrous deeds.
I will delight and rejoice in you;
    I will sing hymns to your name, Most High.
                —Psalm 9:2–3

WHAT IS THIS FORM OF PRAYER?

Devotional prayer has been a part of the Christian tradition since its beginning. While it is distinct from the liturgical celebration, devotional prayer at its best is always inspired by the liturgy and in a sense harmonizes with it, ultimately leading the faithful to a deeper, more reverent participation in the liturgical life of the Church. The earliest Christian communities expressed their love of Christ and the Blessed Mother through prayers and hymns. They honored the martyrs by constructing shrines and churches on the sites of their martyrdom (St. Peter's Basilica and St. Paul's Outside the Walls in Rome are examples) and by visiting these holy places on the anniversaries of their *dies natales*, or birth into eternal life.

Today, devotional prayer encompasses a vast array of prayer practices, and their purpose is indicated in the name of this category—put simply, these prayers are meant to increase one's *devotion*, one's *love* for God. Devotional prayer practices often incorporate the most foundational elements of what it means to be human. They are often rooted in community and family; they include poetry and art and music and dance; they draw upon the rhythms of time and the seasons and celebrate the beauty of nature. Their rich simplicity allows them to become an intensely personal way of expressing one's faith, and their sheer variety allows one to take up different practices over the course of one's life. Whatever circumstances one faces, there is a devotional prayer that will help one reach out to God.

The intimate connection between the devotional life and the liturgy has already been mentioned, but it is important to note that *the liturgy always takes precedence over devotional prayer.* Any form of devotional prayer that encroaches on the liturgy or supersedes it in any way in the imagination or in practice must be avoided. For example, praying the Rosary during Mass was once a fairly common practice generations ago, but this indicates a disordered prioritization of devotional prayer over the liturgical celebration, which deserves the "full, conscious, and active participation" of the faithful (*Sacrosanctum Concilium*, 14). Again, devotional prayer ought to lead to a more fervent participation in the liturgy, not distract from it.

In addition, the connection between the faith of one's heart and the devotional life cannot be overlooked. Devotional prayers and practices are external expressions of an interior disposition of faith; to engage in these prayers or practices without faith reduces them to empty habits, or worse, superstitious behaviors.

WHY MIGHT A PERSON PRAY THIS WAY?

Devotional prayer offers rich possibilities for cultivating one's relationship with God in a way that deeply accords with and reflects one's personality. The devotional life is truly the flowering forth of the graces that are received in the liturgical celebration, and just as there is practically infinite variety in the flowers that grow throughout the world, so too are there practically infinite possibilities for variety within the devotional life. One of the most central forms of devotion in Catholic tradition is prayer to the Blessed Virgin Mary, and yet even within this one subcategory of devotional prayer, numerous possibilities exist: one might choose to pray the Rosary daily, plant a Mary garden in the backyard, reflect on the *Via Matris* (the Way of the Sorrowful Mother) during Lent, or pray at a Marian shrine.

The saints offer even more possibilities: some people may feel a particular closeness to saints whose faith in God was manifested in lives of study; others may be drawn to saints who lived the Gospel in service to the poor and sick or in ceaseless prayer. Devotion to these holy men and women can be expressed through prayer for their intercession, study of their teachings and writings, or imitation of their virtues.

Regardless of the particular shape one's devotional prayer life may take, *all* devotional prayer is ultimately directed toward cultivating one's relationship with God. When we pray to Mary or to the saints and ask their intercession, or when we participate in processions or pilgrimages, we are seeking to grow in our love for God by contemplating his action in the lives of others. When we make a visit to a church to pray before the Blessed Sacrament, we are placing ourselves in God's presence in order to grow closer to him in Christ. When we take up a devotional practice such as wearing the brown scapular or the Miraculous Medal, we are placing upon our bodies a physical reminder that we belong to God, that our lives are not our own, and that we are ever on the journey of faith back to the One who created and redeemed us. Devotional prayers and practices remind us of God's continued presence and action in our lives; they open us up more fully to receive the graces God pours out in the liturgical celebration, and they give everyday expression to the mysteries we celebrate. The liturgy is the root, and the devotional life is the blossom, manifesting the unique beauty of the relationship of love to which God calls each and every person.

WHEN AND WHERE CAN ONE PRACTICE THIS FORM OF PRAYER?

Devotional prayer can be offered at both the individual and communal levels. If you are new to devotional prayer and are uncertain of how you might like to engage in this practice, your parish likely offers opportunities for devotional prayer. These would not only provide a wonderful introduction to the prayer itself, but also help you form relationships with people in your community. For example, the Rosary is often prayed prior to celebrations of Sunday Mass, Stations of the Cross are usually offered during Lent, and Eucharistic Adoration is sometimes made available either at certain times on certain days or, in communities with perpetual adoration chapels, at all times. If your parish or diocese is dedicated to the patronage of a certain saint, there may be opportunities for devotional prayer or even a festival on that saint's feast day. Also, there may be parish or diocesan groups called *sodalities* available in your area where you can join others in prayer.

If you are interested in pursuing devotional prayer privately, you can do so practically anywhere, at any time. Certain devotions are associated with particular days of the week or times of day. For example, the first Friday of each month is dedicated to the Sacred Heart of Jesus, while Saturdays are devoted to honoring the Blessed Mother. The Stations of the Cross are frequently prayed on Fridays

during Lent, and throughout the entire year, devotional prayers
honoring the Passion of Jesus Christ are particularly encouraged
on Fridays at 3:00 p.m., the hour when Jesus died on the Cross.
Other forms of devotional prayer, such as the Angelus, are also tra-
ditionally prayed at certain times (see chapter 3). Novenas (from the
Latin word *novem*, meaning "nine") are a form of devotional prayer
offered for nine consecutive days, derived from the nine days the
Apostles and the Blessed Mother spent together in prayer between
Jesus' Ascension into heaven and the descent of the Holy Spirit on
Pentecost. A novena is typically offered for a particularly pressing
intention; there are numerous novenas addressed to Jesus, the Holy
Spirit, Mary, or saints, often associated with their special patronage.

Other devotional practices can take place within the span of a
moment. For example, simply making the Sign of the Cross before
an important meeting or appointment, when driving or walking
past a church, or when one hears the sirens of an ambulance or
firetruck can be a profound expression of love for God and neighbor.
However, it is particularly important to remember the connection
between faith and devotional practices noted previously. The Sign
of the Cross is a powerful sign of faith; it is not to be made lightly.
Similarly, scapulars, medals, or crucifixes worn around the neck
are not magical talismans; they are sacramentals—signs of faith
meant to cultivate in the wearer a greater openness to God's grace
and a greater fidelity to God's commandments. It is better not to
engage in a devotional practice at all than to do it either thought-
lessly—without any deeper movement of faith in the heart—or
superstitiously—attempting to manipulate a certain outcome as a
kind of spiritual *quid pro quo*. Still, when devotions are chosen with
care and practiced with love and fidelity, they are beautiful ways of
allowing divine light to suffuse everyday life and of making ordinary
moments part of one's relationship with God.

HOW DOES ONE PRAY THIS WAY IN PRACTICE?

Given the profoundly personal nature of devotional prayer, there is no universally applicable way to approach it. Nevertheless, there are some principles to bear in mind as you consider whether to take up a certain form of devotional prayer or practice in your life. First, devotional prayer should arise from and align with who you are at your deepest core; in other words, it should help you express *your* love for God. Pay attention to what aspects of your Catholic faith most resonate with you, and then look for a form of prayer that corresponds to those aspects. If you have a great love for the Eucharist, consider signing up for a regular Holy Hour at your parish. If you are drawn to Our Lady, consider making the Rosary or the Angelus a more consistent part of your prayer life, or see if there are any novenas available that invoke Mary's intercession under a particular title such as Our Lady Undoer of Knots or Our Lady of Sorrows.

Second, the devotional prayers and practices you take up will likely change or evolve throughout your journey of faith. As you learn and grow in your relationship with God, you may be drawn to different devotions. This is normal, and it is indicative of a healthy prayer life. The important thing is to implement change thoughtfully and gradually, rather than flitting from prayer to prayer or practice to practice. Choose your devotions thoughtfully, and commit to them for a set period of time. Within that time, you may experience dryness, but remember that there is grace in remaining faithful to your chosen practice, and know that God will guide you as you consider whether to continue a certain devotion. Finally, and most importantly, devotional prayer is most fruitful when it is rooted in the liturgy. In considering various prayers and practices, take your cue from the prayer of the Church, especially the liturgical year. Many devotions such as the Advent wreath, the Stations of the Cross, or the lesser-known Stations of Light are associated with particular liturgical seasons, and they are powerful ways of entering more fully into the sacred celebration of the liturgy during those times.

If you are ever uncertain about a certain devotional prayer or practice, your pastor or priest can offer guidance, as can a spiritual director. Trusted companions in the faith can help you see whether God might be calling you to a particular devotion or whether it might be time to set a particular prayer or practice aside in order to grow even closer to God through a different form of prayer.

3.

PRAYING THROUGHOUT THE DAY

> From the rising of the sun to its setting
> let the name of the LORD be praised.
>
> —Psalm 113:3

WHAT IS THIS FORM OF PRAYER?

The rhythm of daily life provides many opportunities to turn to God in prayer. Each day—and each moment of each day—is a gift from God, and we can best remind ourselves of this reality by setting aside specific times over the course of each day to *stop* what we're doing, *turn* intentionally to God, and *lift up* in prayer the circumstances in which we find ourselves. In the Old Testament, we see that the Jewish people observed this practice through the prayer known as the Shema, the first line of which is: "Hear, O Israel! The LORD is our God, the LORD alone" (Deuteronomy 6:4).[1] Through his servant Moses, God commanded the people of Israel to pray these words "when you lie down and when you get up" (Deuteronomy 6:7). Even today, devout Jews observe this commandment by praying the Shema at least twice daily. Muslims also pray at five set times each day. It is significant that this practice of praying throughout the day is shared by many major world religions. It speaks to the universal realization that not a single moment of a single day is guaranteed to any person, yet each moment of each day can be received from God as a gift and offered back to God in prayer.

In the Catholic Christian tradition, priests, religious, and many laypeople consecrate their days to God by praying the Liturgy of the Hours (see chapter 1). They join the universal Church in offering psalms and canticles of praise to God primarily at morning, evening, and night, as well as several other times throughout the waking hours of the day. Yet, prior to the development of the Liturgy of the Hours, the earliest Christian communities also prayed to God several times throughout the day, drawing upon the Jewish heritage in which so many of them had been formed. The eighth chapter of a first-century instructional document known as the *Didache*[2] specifies that Christians should pray the Our Father, or Lord's Prayer, three times daily. In addition to the Our Father, the Angelus is another prayer in Catholicism that is prayed at set times throughout the day, traditionally 6:00 a.m., noon, and 6:00 p.m.

WHY MIGHT A PERSON PRAY THIS WAY?

One of the greatest challenges to cultivating a life of prayer is setting aside time for God. In fact, given how busy people are today, this might be *the* greatest challenge, or at least so it seems to those of us who perhaps secretly pride ourselves on being busy. After all, being busy makes us feel important, needed. Staying busy also keeps us from having to confront the still, small voice of God within our hearts that can only be heard in times of quiet and prayer. Busyness run rampant is, at its heart, a manifestation of pride—the busy person has little time for others and perhaps still less time for God. The busy person focuses primarily on his tasks, on her responsibilities, on his ambitions, on her desires. Anything that does not fit in with these self-centered priorities goes by the wayside.

Prayer throughout the day is an antidote to the busy mindset that deludes us into thinking that we are at the center of existence. Taking a few moments for prayer at set times throughout the day is a reality check, for it reminds us that *God* is the center, the ground, the Source of all existence. In prayer, we turn away from ourselves and back toward God, seeking his company and calling to mind the fact that we are always and ever in his presence. When we get wrapped up in the stressful and busy moments of our day, thinking that everything is dependent upon us, even the simplest of prayers offers an opportunity to realign ourselves with the truth that "there is need of only one thing" (Luke 10:42)—to cultivate our relationship with the One who made us, who redeemed us, and who sustains us in every moment of our lives.

Praying at set times throughout the day not only calls to mind our relationship with God; it can also remind us of our relationship with our brothers and sisters. At any given moment of any given day, thousands, perhaps hundreds of thousands, of people throughout the world are praying. By choosing specific times to turn toward God, we can align our prayer with other Christians who might be praying, for example, the Liturgy of the Hours at those same moments. We can also pray in solidarity with people of *all* faiths throughout the world whom we may never meet on this side of eternity, but whom we journey alongside nonetheless as we each make our pilgrimage home to God.

In the simple act of praying at the same time each day, multiple times a day, we come to a deeper appreciation of time itself as a gift from God to be used in cultivating our love for him and for our neighbor. For a few brief moments each day, we set aside those tasks that demand our attention in order to remind ourselves that God is at the heart of everything we do, and the grace that comes from our encounter with him in those moments can in turn transfigure the rest of our tasks and our work into holy offerings, allowing our dialogue with God to overflow from those set times of prayer to fill the rest of our day.

WHEN AND WHERE CAN ONE PRACTICE THIS FORM OF PRAYER?

While there are certain traditions around appropriate times for prayer, you can simply choose the times for prayer that will work best for your particular situation. As you think about how you might incorporate this practice into your spiritual life, first consider how often you would like to turn to God in prayer throughout your day. If setting aside three specific times seems like too much, start with two, and pray when you get up in the morning and before you go to bed at night. If even that is too much right now, just choose one of those two times. The important thing is to choose times that will allow you to be consistent in your prayer. Consistency in prayer will ultimately help nourish a more loving relationship with God.

In terms of where to pray, just as this practice can be done anytime, it can also be done anywhere. Again, consistency is key, so for at least the first few weeks, try to pray in the same place—perhaps in your bedroom in the morning and evening or, if necessary, in a quiet, private space like an office at noon. If privacy at work isn't possible, consider taking a short walk to create an opportunity for you to be alone with God.

Once you commit to this or any other prayer practice, you will likely experience occasional temptations to skip your time of prayer, especially when life is busy. Taking up a spiritual practice is akin to taking up a physical discipline such as running. Just as there will be days you don't want to run, there *will* be times you don't want to pray, even for a few minutes. When you find yourself in this position, be honest with God and with yourself: rather than claiming that you don't have time for prayer, admit that you don't *want* to spend your time in prayer at that particular moment and ask God to help you focus less on yourself and more on him. Then, even if you don't feel like it, do your best to say your chosen prayer anyway.

After praying this way for several weeks or months, you may find yourself longing to increase the number of times you stop what you're doing to turn to God in prayer. This increased desire for prayer is a gift and a grace from God; as Jesus himself taught, "To anyone who has, more will be given" (Matthew 13:12). In other words, the more we pray, the more our desire for God will grow, the more we will want to pray, the more we will pray, and so on. Time given to God is never time wasted. Trust that God himself will guide you as you seek to deepen your relationship with him in prayer.

HOW DOES ONE PRAY THIS WAY IN PRACTICE?

There are as many ways to pray throughout the day as there are prayers in the Christian tradition. Perhaps you are interested in taking up Morning, Evening, or Night Prayer from the Liturgy of the Hours, in which case, as mentioned in chapter 1, there are books or apps available to help you learn this beautiful form of prayer. If you are looking for something simpler, consider one of the two prayers mentioned at the beginning of this chapter: the Lord's Prayer or the Angelus.

The Lord's Prayer

Praying the Lord's Prayer slowly and reverently takes all of thirty to forty-five seconds. Yet, we should not let the simplicity and familiarity of this prayer blind us to its profound power. The Lord's Prayer is the way Jesus responded when his disciples begged him to teach them how to pray (see Luke 11:1ff). The *Catechism* calls it "the fundamental Christian prayer" (*CCC* 2759), and St. Thomas Aquinas deems it "the most perfect of prayers" (*CCC* 2763).[3]

In the Lord's Prayer, we make the words of Jesus our own, thereby expressing our desire to become more like him and to participate in the relationship of love he shares with the Father in the Holy Spirit. Indeed, one could say that the entire life of prayer is contained in the Lord's Prayer, for at its heart, all of Christian prayer is intended to conform us more closely to Jesus Christ, to render us more capable of praying to our Father as he did: "Thy will be done."

When praying the Lord's Prayer at various times throughout the day, give your full attention to the words. If time permits, pause with each intercession as indicated in the line breaks below. Unite your heart to the Sacred Heart of Jesus. Ask him to help you pray this prayer as he intends. Although no set times are named in the *Didache*, praying the Lord's Prayer at morning, at noon, and either in the evening or before going to sleep at night hallows the major segments of the day, allowing you to offer the events unfolding within them to the Father through the words his Son taught us in the grace of the Holy Spirit.

> Our Father who art in heaven,
> hallowed be thy name.
> Thy kingdom come.
> Thy will be done on earth, as it is in heaven.
> Give us this day our daily bread,
> and forgive us our trespasses,

as we forgive those who trespass against us,
and lead us not into temptation,
but deliver us from evil.

The Angelus

Christians have been praying the Hail Mary, or *Ave Maria*, three times per day since at least the twelfth century.[4] The form of the Angelus given below was established by the mid-sixteenth century. In the medieval period, a bell was often rung in the evening from the tower of the local church to signal to the faithful in the surrounding area that it was time to end the workday in prayer. French artist Jean-François Millet (1814–1875) depicts this practice in his moving painting *L'Angelus* (1857–1859), which shows a peasant man and woman standing in a field at dusk, heads bowed and hands folded, their farming implements temporarily laid aside as they stop to pray together.[5]

Like the Lord's Prayer, the Angelus can be prayed in a matter of moments, once, twice, or even three times each day.[6] It is up to each person to discern when and how often they wish to pray the Angelus, taking into account what is possible and reasonable in the course of one's daily schedule. Regardless of when or how often it is prayed, the fruits of this simple practice faithfully undertaken have the capacity to transfigure an entire day, for the Angelus recalls to the one who prays it the mystery of the Incarnation and the humble obedience of the handmaid of the Lord. The one who recalls the Incarnation throughout the day will learn to see the day's events with a new vision—a vision illuminated with the knowledge that "God so loved the world that he gave his only Son" (John 3:16). The Angelus reminds us that "the Word became flesh and made his dwelling among us" (John 1:14), forever changing the course of human history and providing a new orientation for daily life.

V. The angel of the Lord declared unto Mary,

R. and she conceived of the Holy Spirit.

Hail Mary, full of grace, the Lord is with thee. Blessed art thou among women, and blessed is the fruit of thy womb, Jesus. Holy Mary, Mother of God, pray for us sinners, now and at the hour of our death. Amen.

V. Behold, the handmaid of the Lord.

R. Be it done unto me according to thy word.

Hail Mary . . .

V. And the Word was made flesh,[7]

R. and dwelt among us.

Hail Mary . . .

V. Pray for us, O holy Mother of God.

R. That we may be made worthy of the promises of Christ.

Let us pray:

Pour forth, we beseech thee, O Lord, thy grace into our hearts; that we, to whom the Incarnation of Christ, thy Son, was made known by the message of an angel, may, by his Passion and Cross, be brought to the glory of his Resurrection. Through the same Christ our Lord. Amen.

4.

PRAYING WITH SACRED SCRIPTURE

Indeed, the word of God is living and effective, sharper
than any two-edged sword, penetrating even between
soul and spirit, joints and marrow, and able to discern
reflections and thoughts of the heart.

—Hebrews 4:12

WHAT IS THIS FORM OF PRAYER?

In the Christian tradition, praying with scripture[1] is known as *lectio divina*, or "divine reading." It has been practiced by men and women of faith since the early centuries of Christianity, particularly in monastic communities like those founded by St. Benedict of Nursia (ca. 480–550). However, it is important to note at the outset that lectio divina is qualitatively different from any other form of reading a Christian might undertake, even spiritual reading. Lectio divina is a practice of reflecting on the scriptures in such a way that, with the grace of God, reflection becomes meditative prayer, and meditative prayer in turn deepens into contemplative prayer. At its heart, lectio divina is a profound way of nurturing one's relationship with God because it cultivates within the one who practices it a disposition of radical openness, for in this form of prayer, the primary task is that of *listening*.

All too often, prayer can become a soliloquy. Instead of viewing our time spent with God as a fruitful dialogue, we can fall into the habit of doing all the talking, focusing exclusively on our needs, wants, or questions. While we should never hesitate to bring these before God, we must also remember that we can only hear God speak to us when we fall silent in his presence. One cannot hear God's "still, small voice" if one never listens for it (see 1 Kings 19:12).

Lectio divina teaches us to "be still" and know that God is God, and we are not (see Psalm 46:11). In the midst of our need, the Word of God speaks of comfort. In the times of our confusion, it shows us the path forward. In the depths of our suffering, it promises new life. And yet, the converse is also true: in our complacency, the Word of God exhorts us to vigilance; in our indifference, it urges action; in our sinfulness, it calls for repentance. Thus, the disposition of openness necessary for a fruitful practice of lectio divina is in fact an *openness to conversion*. To engage in lectio divina is to cede control over one's time of prayer and say to God, "Speak, Lord, for your servant is listening" (1 Samuel 3:9), all the while knowing that the Word of God is "sharper than any two-edged sword" (Hebrews 4:12). There is real risk in this, but there is also real reward, for in praying with the scriptures in particular, we encounter the One who has "the words of eternal life" (John 6:68). The more we meditate and pray with the scriptures, the more these words of eternal life become the lens through which we view the events of our lives. The more time we spend with the Word of God, the more we will be conformed to the One who reveals himself in it.

WHY MIGHT A PERSON PRAY THIS WAY?

According to the teachings of the Second Vatican Council, "In the sacred books [of the scriptures], the Father who is in heaven meets his children with great love and speaks with them" (*Dei Verbum*, 21). This is a profoundly beautiful truth. The words of scripture are the words God himself speaks to us, his children. So many people today are searching high and low for God's presence in their lives; they only need to take the Bible down from the shelf where it has likely been gathering dust, open it, and immerse themselves in the story of God's love for them. Far from being antiquated words with no applicability to modern life, the Word of God in scripture is how we come to understand life itself. By contemplating in prayer the narrative of salvation history recorded in scripture, we come to a deeper understanding of God's action in the narratives of our own lives.

Lectio divina is also a practice that may appeal to those who struggle against the busyness and distractibility of life today. Its slow, reflective, collected pace runs counter to the practices of skimming and scrolling encouraged by frequent internet use. At the same time, given the shallow, superficial way most reading is undertaken today, lectio divina may present a challenge to some. In a culture that prizes endless novelty, lectio divina's emphasis on repetition may seem pointless, but it is a practice of prayer firmly rooted in the idea of "quality over quantity." Each repetition is like a plane passing over a rough plank of wood, or a small stream flowing over rock. Over time, the wood's rough edges are made smooth and the water shapes even the hardest stone.

Repetition is in fact the key to lectio divina, because the riches of scripture are inexhaustible. We will never grasp their full depths after the first reading, or the second reading, or even the ninety-second reading, because the scriptures are the Word of God, and God is inexhaustible mystery. Yet, precisely through repetition, we can plumb the depths of inexhaustible mystery further and further, growing in intimacy with and love for the One who comes to meet and speak with us in the scriptures. Gradually, this repeated meditation on the Word of God may give way to simply contemplating God himself in a spirit of loving communion that is beyond words. Thus, lectio divina is a powerful gateway to contemplative prayer.

Additionally, by calling forth an openness to conversion, lectio divina is also an effective guide for living out the teachings of Jesus Christ. By opening ourselves up to the Word of God in meditation and prayer, we also open ourselves up to the promptings of the Holy Spirit, whose inspirations fan the spark of divine love in our hearts into a flame, conforming us to Christ by burning away our impurities in the crucible of prayer, showing us how God is calling us to become witnesses to the truth of scripture as living words of the Word.

WHEN AND WHERE CAN ONE PRACTICE THIS FORM OF PRAYER?

Once again, consistency is key in the practice of lectio divina. In terms of time, many of its proponents recommend praying lectio divina first thing in the morning, when the mind is rested and refreshed, before the demands of the day have asserted themselves. However, this may not be possible in every case; therefore, it is up to each person to consider thoughtfully and prayerfully what time will be the most realistic for his or her particular situation. In terms of duration, the most important thing to remember is that one should not rush through lectio divina. At a bare minimum, fifteen minutes should be set aside for praying in this way; ideally, that time frame will be longer—anywhere from thirty to forty-five minutes. Remember, this reading is qualitatively different from any other reading, because this reading is also prayer. The Word of God will not have the chance to take root deep within your heart if the time you spend meditating on it is rushed or perfunctory. Be generous with your time, and be patient in your prayer.

Some Christians practice lectio divina in community, gathering in homes or meeting at the parish, proclaiming and re-proclaiming the scripture passage slowly and in turn, listening attentively together to the Word of God, and progressing at their own pace through the various stages described below. This way of praying lectio divina may or may not involve sharing the insights one receives in prayer with the group, or it may simply provide a kind of accountability for maintaining one's commitment to the practice of praying with scripture. The important thing to remember is that lectio divina isn't the same thing as Bible study, though it would be an appropriate way to conclude such a gathering. Rather, lectio divina is a practice of prayer in which we spend time growing closer to God by meditating on how he has revealed himself in scripture.

Other Christians practice lectio divina on a private, individual basis. In this case, as with other forms of prayer, it is best to create a setting that minimizes the possibility for distractions and enhances one's openness to the Word of God. A candle may serve as a symbol for the enlightenment we seek in approaching scripture. An icon of Jesus Christ may remind us of the Word Incarnate, to whom all the scriptures point. A beautiful edition of the Bible will encourage the proper reverence toward God who is present in his Word and remind us that we are on holy ground when we approach the scriptures.

HOW DOES ONE PRAY THIS WAY IN PRACTICE?

The first step in lectio divina is choosing a passage from scripture. Those just beginning in this practice may wish to choose one of the daily readings from the Mass, or a psalm or canticle from the Liturgy of the Hours.[2] It is in the liturgical prayer of the Church that the scriptures find their fullest expression; thus, allowing the liturgy to direct one's lectio divina not only strengthens the awareness of the connection between the liturgy and scripture but also disposes one to celebrate the liturgy more fruitfully.

Another possibility in choosing a reading for lectio divina is to prayerfully select one book from the Bible and progress through it slowly, day by day, a few verses at a time. This respects the integrity of the scriptural text and prevents the possibility of skipping over verses or sections that may be spiritually challenging. Any of the synoptic Gospels (Matthew, Mark, or Luke) would be a good first choice for lectio divina. Whatever book you choose, what is essential in lectio divina is to give yourself over to the Word of God: instead of praying with your favorite passages only, commit to humbly receiving the Word of God, either from the liturgy or in the context of an entire biblical book. Open yourself up to being both comforted and confronted by God's Word. Do not worry that you may not know the historical context or the literary genre of a particular passage or book. While this information is important and can deepen your understanding of scripture, it is not a prerequisite in order to pray with the Word of God. Lectio divina is not reserved for scripture scholars. It is for every person of faith and good will who desires to encounter and be led by God in the words he has spoken to his children.

While lectio divina has been part of the Christian prayer tradition for more than a millennium, the stages below were formulated in the twelfth century by Guigo the Carthusian (d. 1188). Once a passage is chosen, prior to beginning lectio divina, it is important to take as much time as necessary to quiet your mind and prepare your heart, asking God to open the scriptures for you as Christ did for the disciples on the road to Emmaus (see Luke 24:13–35). Then you may mark the end of your preparation and the beginning of lectio divina with a verse from scripture offered in prayer, such as "Speak, for your servant is listening" (1 Samuel 3:10), "You have the words of eternal life" (John 6:68), or "Your word is a lamp for my feet, a light for my path" (Psalm 119:105). Continue by progressing through the steps below.

1. *Lectio* (reading): Read the passage aloud, slowly. Vocalizing the words will automatically slow your reading pace, and you may find that you naturally emphasize certain words within the passage. Pause after this initial reading, noting the words or phrases that your voice intuitively accented or lingered over, or those that resonated within your heart.

2. *Meditatio* (meditation): Read the passage aloud again, preserving the same reflective pace as before. Meditation is often described as a kind of rumination, "chewing" on the text as a cow chews its cud—visiting the text again and again so as to digest and assimilate its meaning more and more fully. Do not be in a hurry to rush past this reflective meditation on the text; let it sink down deep into your heart and mind as you continue to turn over particular words or phrases, considering their meaning.

3. *Oratio* (prayer): Read the passage aloud a third time, even more slowly than before, allowing yourself to continue acclimating to the sacred pace of scripture. Engage in a dialogue with the

text, and with God, who is speaking to you through the text. Ask yourself what God might be trying to say to you, what invitation God might be extending to you. Consider what the text might be telling you about yourself, and share your response with God. You may find it helpful to write these thoughts in a journal, committing to words your dialogue with the Word.

4. *Contemplatio* (contemplation): Read the passage aloud a final time, giving yourself over to it as completely as possible, surrendering to God the words or phrases that have resonated with you in your time of prayer and the responses or questions that have arisen. Simply allow yourself to be still. Rest in the loving embrace of God.

To mark the conclusion of this time of intimate conversation with God, offer a prayer of praise or thanksgiving, perhaps an Our Father or Glory Be. Ask God to preserve in your heart the spirit of openness in which you have spent this time, so that you might allow the Word to take flesh in your life as you continue pondering your scripture passage throughout your day.

For those who are seeking immediate, easy answers, lectio divina can be a challenging way to pray; nevertheless, its fruits for the patient practitioner are as inexhaustible as scripture itself. The more you search for God in the scriptures, the more you will find God there, and the more God will guide you to seek him even more ardently.

5.

PRAYING THROUGH EXPERIENCE

LORD you have probed me, you know me:
> you know when I sit and stand;
> you understand my thoughts from afar.
You sift through my travels and my rest;
> with all my ways you are familiar.
Even before a word is on my tongue,
> LORD, you know it all.

—Psalm 139:1–4

WHAT IS THIS FORM OF PRAYER?

Praying through one's experiences has been practiced in the Catholic Christian tradition for centuries, but the specific form we will explore in this chapter is known as the Examen, which can be found in the teachings of St. Ignatius of Loyola (1491–1556), founder of the Society of Jesus (the Jesuit order). If prayer is a relationship with God, then the Examen can be thought of as a daily check-in conversation with God. For Ignatius, the Examen occupied an indispensable place in his life of prayer, and he constantly encouraged others to take up the practice as well. In his *Spiritual Exercises*, Ignatius teaches that the Examen should be prayed twice each day—at midday and in the evening—as a way of remaining in consistent

51

dialogue with God, even (and perhaps especially) in the seemingly insignificant moments of one's daily life.

In this form of prayer, we reflect on the events of our day and bring them before God in a spirit of humility and gratitude. We ask for the wisdom to see our lives as God does, for forgiveness for those times when we've failed to be the person God has created and called us to be, and for courage and strength to live as a more faithful disciple moving forward. As with all prayer, the emphasis here is not so much on our action in reviewing the events of our day, but on *God's action* as he fills us with a deeper awareness of his presence in past events and guides us to a greater understanding of where he desires to lead us in the future.

The gift of the Examen is that it cultivates within those who pray it a spirit of attentiveness or mindfulness. Fr. Timothy Gallagher, O.M.V., calls it "a prayer of spiritual awareness."[1] As one becomes more practiced in bringing the events of the day before God at certain times, one begins to notice God's presence more as those events unfold in real time, and one becomes more capacitated to respond in the moment to those events as God desires. Growth in our attentiveness to and awareness of God's presence throughout our day, like all spiritual growth, takes time. It requires patience with ourselves, patience with God, and fidelity to the practice of searching out God's presence in our everyday lives. Nevertheless, we can take heart and have confidence in pursuing God through this form of prayer, for we would not be seeking God in the first place if God had not already found us.

WHY MIGHT A PERSON PRAY THIS WAY?

Those learning about the Examen for the first time may be skeptical about its offer of developing spiritual clarity, wondering whether this might be too good to be true. Like all prayer, what the Examen offers is a path to reforming and conforming our vision to God's, and in this instance, the path consists of our daily experiences. When we pray the Examen, we come before God precisely from wherever we might be in our lives, and we ask God to help us look at our experiences from the divine point of view. It bears repeating that God knows us better than we know ourselves, loves us more than we love ourselves, and desires communion with us far more than we desire communion with him, so the *only* way for us to begin to understand the events of our lives is to bring them before God and ask for the grace of illumination.

Praying the Examen is a simple way to grow in relationship with God. It's like coming home to a loved one at the end of a long day—describing the moments that lifted our spirits and those that tried our patience, sharing the times when we felt as if we were exactly the person we're meant to be and the times when we failed miserably, confiding the hopes and dreams we have for our future and discerning how best to make them a reality. Yet this simple practice can be challenging, too. It demands that we look at ourselves with humility and honesty. We cannot gloss over certain moments in the day or sweep others under the rug, hoping to hide them from God. As such, praying the Examen requires profound courage, for over time and with God's grace, we will learn to see our lives as they truly are. And more often than not, this will require us to change in some way. Still, we will also learn to see God's infinite patience with us, the tender love of the One who gently guides us toward himself through the simple, ordinary *stuff* that makes up our lives—and we will not only learn to respond to this divine guidance, but the more we pray, the more we will *desire* to respond in love.

WHEN AND WHERE CAN ONE PRACTICE THIS FORM OF PRAYER?

St. Ignatius advised that the Examen be prayed twice a day, at midday and in the evening, but it can also be prayed first thing in the morning, while reflecting on the previous day's events. As with all prayer, thoughtful discernment is necessary as you determine what will work best, both in terms of how often you pray the Examen and when you pray it. If you feel drawn to the Examen, commit to praying it once per day at first, for ten to fifteen minutes. After some time, you may decide either to lengthen your time in prayer, or to add a second Examen to your day, but in general, when seeking to create any new habit or practice, it's best to start small.

Begin by taking an honest inventory of your day to determine the most opportune time(s) to pray the Examen. If your workday leaves you exhausted in the evening, then consider making a midday Examen over your lunch break. If family obligations require your attention until your children are in bed, then perhaps an early morning Examen before they wake up will work best for you. If you prefer to look back over an entire day's events, then praying the Examen at night may be the best option. Some schedules permit people to pray the Examen at the same time each day; other schedules require more flexibility. The important thing is to choose a time when you are fully awake and alert.

The same careful consideration is also needed in choosing where to pray your Examen. A busy professional may have the option of closing the office door, while a parent of young children may have to resort to the privacy of the bathroom. Someone with a sedentary routine may choose to pray the Examen while taking a walk, whereas someone with a physically demanding job may prefer the comfort of a favorite armchair. Praying in a chapel before Jesus present in the Blessed Sacrament is also a beautiful way to practice the Examen. Regardless of when and where you choose to pray it, the Examen will provide a grace-filled opportunity to bring the events of your daily life to God. In the process, it will help you to discern how God is always present in those events, calling you lovingly to grow closer to him.

HOW DOES ONE PRAY THIS WAY IN PRACTICE?

The Examen proper comprises the five steps given below, but St. Ignatius also recommended times of transition before and after making the Examen. The first transition facilitates a more recollected entrance into the time of prayer; the second transition facilitates a more prayerful entrance back into the demands of the day.[2] You may choose to mark the beginning of your Examen by inviting God to guide your prayer with a brief phrase like "Come, Holy Spirit" and to conclude with the Lord's Prayer or a Glory Be to thank God for this time of prayerful conversation and reflection.

Step 1: Gratitude

Begin the Examen by naming the gifts God has given you and thanking God for them. As noted in the discussion on prayers of thanksgiving in the introduction, gratitude is the hallmark of the Christian life. It places us in right relationship with God because by it we acknowledge that everything in life—including life itself—is sheer gift, and that God is the Source and Giver of all gifts. Gratitude is the humble prayer of the creature to her Creator. It allows her to see and know herself as infinitely loved by the One who will never hesitate to provide for her and who is always at work in her life.

Step 2: Petition

Ask God to illuminate your heart and help you be attentive to where he is working in your life, and where he is leading you. With its central focus on reviewing the events of daily life, there is a risk that the Examen might erroneously be perceived primarily as our effort. This second step acknowledges the primacy of God's action in our time of prayer: only with God's grace can we hope to *perceive* the events of our lives rightly and *respond* to them in accordance with God's will for us.

Step 3: Review

Look back over the events of your day. Ignatius recommends doing so "hour by hour, or from one period of time to another."[3] As you do so, note the moments when you felt particularly close to or far away from God, moments when you felt inner peace or inner turmoil. Consider the moments when God may have been inviting you to draw closer to him and whether you responded to that invitation by accepting or rejecting it. Ask yourself honestly whether your heart has been open to God's will today or resistant to it.

Step 4: Forgiveness

Ask God to forgive you for the times throughout the day when you've fallen short. An honest review of the day's events in step 3 will inevitably reveal to us moments when we failed in our calling as Christians to love God and neighbor, to love as Christ loves us. And yet, if we remember that God's love for us is infinite, then it follows that God's mercy toward us is boundless. Any relationship of love is deepened and strengthened by forgiveness sought and received. Our relationship with God is no different. When we lay our failures at God's feet and humbly ask for forgiveness, we become like the sinful woman in the Gospel of Luke who anointed Jesus' feet, who shows him great love precisely *because* her many sins were forgiven (see Luke 7:36–50).

Step 5: Response

Determine how you will put the insights God has given you in prayer into action, with the help of God's grace. Whether you pray the Examen in the morning, at midday, or at night, this final step provides a path forward once the formal time of prayer has concluded. Most often, the responses God calls forth in us will be small. Perhaps we make a simple resolution: "When my child has a tantrum, I will take a deep breath and pray, 'Come, Holy Spirit,' before responding." Or: "When my coworker gossips about someone else, I will disengage from the conversation instead of adding fuel to the fire." Over time, these small responses become slow but steady progress in the spiritual life—progress rooted in seeking God's presence in each and every moment of the day.

In praying the Examen, you may find that you spend more time on one step than on others. There is no set rule for how much time ought to be spent on each part of the Examen; if you genuinely ask the Holy Spirit's guidance in your prayer, you will know when it is time to progress to the next step. However, if you find yourself wanting to skip or rush past a particular step, it is best to stop and consider why this is the case. Perhaps you experienced a rock-bottom moment in your day that you would rather forget about. Perhaps you are struggling to ask God's forgiveness for a sinful habit.

Resistance is often a sign that something deep is at work, and though these interior struggles can be painful to address, the Divine Physician promises light and healing to all who ask it of him.

Many people use journaling to help them process their Examen, as writing is often an incredibly useful tool for gaining clarity. However, should the self-reflection practiced in the Examen raise deep issues to the surface, one should never hesitate to seek the help of a trusted spiritual director or companion, or, if necessary, a therapist or mental-health professional. While coupling the Examen with spiritual direction is not an absolute requirement, it is highly recommended. The care and guidance of someone well-versed in the spiritual life can help make sense of the insights received in the Examen and provide counsel for how to put them into practice.

6.

PRAYING THROUGH BEAUTY

The heavens declare the glory of God;
　　the firmament proclaims the works of his hands.
　　　　　　　　　　　　　　　　　　—Psalm 19:2

WHAT IS THIS FORM OF PRAYER?

In this chapter and the next, we will be exploring not forms of prayer *per se*, but aids to prayer. The first of these is beauty. The beauty of creation speaks of the love of the Creator; as such, engaging with beauty can help deepen one's practices of prayer as one seeks to grow in relationship with the One who is Beauty itself. In this chapter, we will focus on the beauty of nature, the beauty of visual art, and the beauty of music. All authentic beauty—in other words, all beauty that conveys truth and evokes a desire for goodness in the viewer—is a reflection of God's own beauty. Yet, in a fallen world, there exists the possibility that beauty may be misused or misunderstood, that it may become an *idol*, an end unto itself, rather than an *icon*, which points beyond itself to God. Still, the rich heritage of the arts throughout the history of Christianity teaches us that we should not fear or hesitate to incorporate beauty into our prayer, so long as we do so not for its own ends, but for the express purpose of praising God.

Nature

Anyone who has stood on the shore of the ocean, watched a magnif-
icent sunrise, or gazed up at the brilliance of a star-strewn night sky
has undoubtedly been moved by the beauty of creation. Apart from
the stunning landscapes, there are the creatures themselves—from
the delicate butterfly to the majestic lion to the immense blue whale,
culminating in the awe-inspiring mystery of each human person.
Creation is astounding. The psalmist shows us the right response to
nature and how it can become a catalyst for prayer:

> Oh LORD, our Lord,
>> how awesome is your name through all the earth!
>
> I will sing of your majesty above the heavens. . . .
>
> When I see your heavens, the work of your fingers,
>> the moon and stars that you set in place—
> What is man that you are mindful of him,
>> and a son of man that you care for him?
> Yet you have made him little less than a god,
>> crowned him with glory and honor,
> You have given him rule over the works of your hands,
>> put all things at his feet:
> All sheep and oxen,
>> even the beasts of the field,
> The birds of the air, the fish of the sea,
>> and whatever swims the paths of the seas.
>
> O LORD, our Lord,
>> how awesome is your name through all the earth!
>> —Psalm 8:2, 4–10

The psalmist's experience of nature first inspires humility: he marvels
at the fact that the same God who created the earth and heavens

also created humanity in the divine image and likeness (see Genesis 1:26), placing human beings in authority over the created world. The psalmist responds to this realization with a prayer of praise, proclaiming the Lord's name throughout the earth. We, too, are called to praise God for all he has created and to express our gratitude for God's creation by caring for it as stewards, exercising rightly the authority God has given to us.

Visual Art

In addition to the beauty of creation, the beauty of visual art can also serve as a powerful aid to prayer, particularly when it depicts sacred or religious subject matter. St. John Damascene (d. 749), who defended the Church's use of images during the iconoclastic controversy of the eighth century, affirmed that "the beauty and color of images are stimuli to prayer; they offer a feast for the eyes, just as the spectacle of the countryside spurs my heart to glorify God."[1] Visual representations of Christ, Mary, and the saints are by no means idols, which are images that are worshipped in and of themselves. Rather, they are intended to direct the mind and the heart beyond the image to the actual *person* represented and to inspire a deeper devotion for that person and for God, whose love is made manifest in that person. When we look at a photograph of a loved one, we grow in love not for the photo, but for the person *in* the photo. Similarly, an image of Jesus ought to inspire a deeper love in us—not for the image, but for Jesus himself.

Visual art can form an integral part of one's devotional prayer life, for it engages the imagination in a vivid way as one contemplates the mysteries of faith and the realities of God's love. For example, one can hardly look at even a photograph of Michelangelo's *Pietà*—let alone the real sculpture—without being deeply moved by the intensely human representation of Mary cradling the dead Christ in her lap.[2] Yet, the remarkable humanity of Michelangelo's master-piece is also suffused with a radiance that points to the divine: the serene expression of the Virgin, the positioning of Jesus' Body, and the relationship between the two figures not only evokes an emotional pathos within the viewer, but it can also deepen the viewer's spiritual understanding of what it means to profess that Jesus died for our salvation.

Gazing at a beautiful work of sacred visual art can lead to a contemplation of God that goes beyond images; such art encourages a movement from the external to the internal and from the internal to the eternal—from seeing with one's physical eyes to seeing with the eyes of faith. When one is able to pierce beyond the veil of a beautiful image to the reality it represents, an encounter with the Source of all beauty takes place, and one is made aware of the call to become beautiful in the eyes of God.

Music

There is no doubt that music has an incredible capacity to move the heart, so it is only right that it should be considered another powerful aid to prayer alongside nature and visual art. Yet, vocal music in particular is unique among the three kinds of beauty discussed in this chapter: when we sing the words of scripture or the texts of the Mass or other prayers, then vocal music actually *does* become prayer itself, not just something that might aid or inspire prayer. Not only that, but music elevates and ennobles a text, giving words a meaning that transcends what speech alone can convey. As a result, when we sing our prayers, they take on an intensity and a fervor beyond what they would have had if we had simply spoken them. The well-known phrase attributed to St. Augustine illustrates this mysterious reality perfectly: "The one who sings prays twice."

Music-making is a deeply human act. It permeates everyday life and allows us to mark special occasions. We sing our children to sleep and improvise harmonies on the final phrase of "Happy Birthday"; we belt fight songs to cheer on our team and make mixes or playlists of special songs for the people we love. It makes sense, then, that music should also permeate and punctuate our relationship of prayer with God. Imagine a wedding without a majestic fanfare to accompany the newlyweds' exit, or a funeral without a hymn of peace and comfort. Imagine celebrating Christmas without singing "O Come, All Ye Faithful" or "O Holy Night" or "Hark! The Herald Angels Sing," or participating in the Good Friday celebration without hearing "Were You There When They Crucified My Lord?" Whatever the context, music deepens meaning.

Music also fills the life of prayer at an even more foundational level by serving as a mnemonic device, helping us to remember how to respond to God. It is far easier to sing the Glory to God at Mass than to simply speak it! The melody and rhythm and harmony etch the words more firmly into our memories and our hearts, carrying the prayer forward long after the music has ended. How often have we found ourselves humming the final hymn from Mass well into Sunday evening, or perhaps recalling the melody of the Responsorial Psalm throughout the week? Joining the words of our prayers to music enriches our prayers. It intensifies them. It brings them to life in a way beyond our comprehension, and it helps us to enter more fully into our relationship with God.

Instrumental music can also enhance our life of prayer, though not in the same way that vocal music does. In this regard, instrumental music is more akin to natural beauty or visual art as a catalyst of prayer, though it still possesses a quality that sets it apart from these other forms of beauty. When we listen to or perform instrumental music, we are in a very real sense taken out of our own time and immersed into music's time. To respect the integrity of a musical work, we must make the entire journey through it, from beginning to middle to end. As such, music requires a certain giving over of the self, an acceptance of its interior logic and order and a submission of our own. This giving over of the self is precisely what must happen in the life of prayer: we must set aside our agendas and our expectations and open ourselves up to the logic and order and love of God. We progress in the spiritual life not necessarily by moving at the pace we would choose or even desire, but by opening ourselves up to God's action within our hearts and humbly submitting to God's pace and God's timing. There are no shortcuts through a piece of music, and there are no shortcuts through the spiritual life. Thus, because music is such a profound reminder of these mysterious spiritual realities, it is well worth incorporating into one's life of prayer.

WHY MIGHT A PERSON PRAY THIS WAY?

Beauty makes us more authentically human. It forms us in the act of beholding; it renders us capable of wonder. An authentic encounter with beauty is always self-emptying, because when we see or hear something beautiful, our focus is on that something beautiful, and not on ourselves. When we forget ourselves, we become open to being transformed by that which we encounter. Beauty teaches us to see beyond ourselves. It even beckons us to see beyond itself to discover a richer level of meaning and a higher plane of existence.

For the Christian, earthly beauty is a reflection and a manifestation of God's beauty, which is revealed most fully in Jesus Christ, who is "the image [icon] of the invisible God" (Colossians 1:15). God calls us to himself through the beauty of all that he has created, so it is only right that we respond to that call by incorporating the beauty God has given us into our life of prayer and participating in it whenever possible (as in the act of singing during Mass). When we struggle to find God in the midst of our own circumstances, the beauty of the created world can remind us of the divine order that exists at the heart of all things and sustains everything in being, including ourselves. When we grapple with the mysteries of the Christian faith, a work of visual art can enlighten our minds and strengthen our belief. When we cannot express the joy or the pain we are experiencing, music can give voice to our most heartfelt prayers and deepen the intimacy of our relationship with God.

WHEN AND WHERE CAN ONE PRACTICE THIS FORM OF PRAYER?

The beauty of creation can always be accessed and incorporated into prayer, even if it's just taking a moment to look out a window on a snowy day or stand in the yard watching the sun set. All it takes is an intentional act of the will.

The worlds of visual art and music are endlessly accessible and easily searchable through the internet, which can be a great gift as you begin to explore them; however, it would be a mistake to *only* engage these forms of beauty online. As you read the suggestions below, be sure to seek out possibilities in your area that would allow you to thoughtfully incorporate art and music into your prayer life in an in-person, incarnational way whenever possible, rather than through exclusively virtual means.

HOW DOES ONE PRAY THIS WAY IN PRACTICE?

Each person's response to beauty is different, so each person's engagement with and incorporation of beauty into prayer will vary, but a few general suggestions are offered here.

Nature

You don't have to travel to the Grand Canyon or swim in the Pacific Ocean to appreciate the beauty of nature. (Though if you can, by all means, do so!) Simply taking a leisurely walk through your neighborhood without your smartphone or earbuds is enough, as long as you take the time to *notice* the beauty around you. Look at the trees. Observe where they are in their cycle of bud, bloom, decay, or dormancy. Search for squirrels or chipmunks or other wildlife. Listen for birdsong. Breathe deeply and notice any aromas that might be wafting on the air. Engage as many of your senses as you can, and take a moment to recall that everything around you was created by the same God who wants to be in relationship with you.

If you live in a big city and are unable to spend time in nature, consider bringing a few plants into your home environment, especially into the space where you pray. Plants, flowers, or even candles made from natural substances such as beeswax serve as reminders of God's abounding generosity and love in the gift of creation.

Visual Art

To enjoy beautiful visual art, visit a local or nearby museum—and be sure to spend time in any gallery where sacred or religious art is on display. If geographical or financial constraints make a museum visit impossible, check out books on religious art from your local library. Another simple possibility is to visit a beautiful church in your diocese and spend time just *looking*.[3] Churches have long been home to some of humanity's most stunning works of visual art: the beauty of the art and architecture was intended to proclaim the riches of the faith to all who crossed the threshold and to draw people into the mysteries of God. Marveling at the beauty of the physical space, we recall that we are in God's house, on holy ground, and so the step from pondering to prayer becomes simple and natural. Finally, consider choosing a sacred image or two to display in your home. An icon, a reproduction of a religious painting, a crucifix, or a small statue can become a catalyst for prayer or devotional practice—perhaps each time the image catches your eye, you can say a brief prayer like "Glory to you, O Lord," or "Jesus, remember me." Or perhaps you can venerate your crucifix or icon with a kiss before going to bed. If you have a dedicated space for prayer, consider changing your art with the liturgical season—a Nativity scene for Advent and Christmas, a Crucifixion scene for Lent and the Triduum, a Resurrection scene for Easter, and your favorite image of Jesus for Ordinary Time. Such changes will prevent your engagement with art from stagnating over time and will prompt new occasions and inspirations for prayer.

Music

Incorporating music into your personal prayer doesn't require any musical training or specialized knowledge. Recordings of sacred music of all styles are widely available online, but searching the entire internet for something that resonates with you can feel a lot like searching for the proverbial needle in a haystack that is also made of needles. Hopefully you have had at least a basic level of exposure to sacred music through participating in Sunday Mass and therefore know what speaks to your heart, but if you genuinely have no idea where to begin (or if your experience of music at Mass has been somewhat lacking), the music of the Taizé community can be a gentle point of entry into sacred devotional music. Taizé music is simply constructed, often featuring a refrain that serves as a repeated mantra throughout the piece. This repetitive structure makes the music easy to learn and serves as an effective memory aid, rooting the words and melody deep in one's heart so that the prayer can be called to mind at any time. Another possibility for discovering new sacred music is to search for settings of scriptural texts that are meaningful for you personally. Many psalms in particular have been set to music often over the past several centuries, as have Gospel canticles such as the Magnificat (Luke 1:46–55).

When it comes to deciding when and how to bring music into your time of prayer, the Mass can serve as a helpful model. Music often marks the beginning and the conclusion of the eucharistic celebration and accompanies times of prayerful reflection. You may choose to begin or end your time of prayer with a favorite hymn. Even if you're convinced that you don't have the best voice, don't be afraid to sing. You might also consider listening to a piece of sacred music as a way of reflecting on a passage of scripture. Whether you are praying alone or with others, music is a beautiful way to elevate your prayer and enrich your relationship with God.

As a final note, enjoying God's gift of beauty is an invitation to prayer for all Christians. For the Christian artist, musician, or craftsperson, the gift of *making* something beautiful is a special invitation to participate in the loving creativity of God. Practicing our own creativity can also become a catalyst for prayer when we first recall that God is the Source of our gifts and talents, and then seek to glorify God by using those gifts and talents in his service, helping other people to pray and praise him.

7.

PRAYING THROUGH THE BODY

> Do you not know that your body is a temple of the holy Spirit within you, whom you have from God, and that you are not your own? For you have been purchased at a price. Therefore glorify God in your body.
> —1 Corinthians 6:19–20

WHAT IS THIS FORM OF PRAYER?

In this chapter, as in chapter 6, we will be examining not a form of prayer, but practices that can help to enrich one's life of prayer. It may seem odd to think about the body when it comes to prayer; as human beings, we do nothing outside of our bodies, so of course all prayer happens in the body. Yet just as we can draw closer to God through the particularity of the mind by nourishing our intellect in study and reflection, so too the body and its particularity can become an instrument that helps us grow in our understanding and love of God. We will consider two ways in which God's gift of our bodies may help to facilitate deeper prayer: movement—specifically making pilgrimage—and fasting. Both of these practices are rooted in *asceticism*, which is a kind of physical discipline undertaken for a spiritual purpose.

Pilgrimage

How might different kinds of movement help us turn to God in prayer? In the Christian tradition, going on pilgrimage has long been an honored practice by which a person might grow closer to God. A pilgrimage is a special journey to a holy shrine or city, undertaken for the express purpose of spiritual growth and renewal. The journey of faith itself is often described as a pilgrimage; similarly, the *Catechism* affirms that "pilgrimages evoke our earthly journey toward heaven" (*CCC* 2691). With the increase in global mobility, many Christians throughout the world are making pilgrimages as a way of growing in their relationship with God. However, there is always a risk that a pilgrimage may devolve into mere vacation, where one might "tour" a few holy places. Prayer and asceticism keep this from happening. While one's particular practices of prayer may not necessarily change during a pilgrimage, the lens through which one views them does. For example, it is one thing to offer a prayer like the Rosary in the home; it is quite another to pray it while on pilgrimage. In the latter context, the rhythm of repeated prayers may set our walking or climbing pace, and the pilgrimage site may bring our meditations to life in a new and different way: imagine praying a mystery like the Carrying of the Cross while walking up a steep hill to a shrine.

Many well-established pilgrimage sites are also associated with a physical discipline beyond merely walking toward a particular location or giving up comfortable accommodations. For example, pilgrims ascend Rome's *Scala Sacra* (Sacred Stairs) on their knees as they pray. Those climbing Croagh Patrick, or St. Patrick's Mountain, located outside Dublin, Ireland, traditionally make the journey barefoot, and some pilgrims specifically choose to make this journey during colder seasons in order to increase its physical difficulty in the hopes that it might bear greater fruit in their spiritual lives.

Fasting

Perhaps more familiar and accessible than making a pilgrimage, fasting—choosing to abstain from some sort of material good, often food or drink—is another way that the body becomes an instrument to help one draw closer to God in prayer. There are many mentions of fasting in the Bible: Moses neither ate nor drank for forty days when he was on Mount Horeb receiving the Ten Commandments from God (see Deuteronomy 9:9), the citizens of Nineveh fasted in response to Jonah's preaching (see Jonah 3:5), and Jesus himself fasted in the desert for forty days and nights after being baptized in the Jordan by John (see Matthew 4:2). Today, Lent is the liturgical season most Christians associate with fasting, but it can be undertaken at any time. Indeed, the current obligatory Lenten fasts from meat on Fridays were once observed year-round in the Church, and many Christians today continue this practice.

Like pilgrimages, there is always a possibility that fasting may become an end in itself rather than a means of nourishing one's relationship with God. Because of these risks, one must always begin discerning any ascetical practice with a serious examination of one's motivations for doing so. Are you giving up chocolate for Lent as a physical discipline aimed at spiritual growth, or is it part of an effort to lose weight? Is your desire to forsake all food on Fridays driven by a desire to imitate Jesus' fast, or because you think such a radical gesture is necessary in order to "earn" his love? Are you abstaining from alcohol in order to give the money you would have spent to the poor, or because it will impress your friends? Fasting can be a great gift to one's spiritual life, but done for the wrong reasons, it can become an immense obstacle to growing in relationship with God.

In recent years, intermittent fasting has become increasingly popular: people undertake this practice with the goal of increasing mental clarity or boosting the metabolism. There is nothing wrong with fasting to obtain these physical benefits, but for the Christian, fasting can only be *spiritually* beneficial if it is oriented toward prayer.

Finally, there is also a risk that fasting may be misunderstood as a kind of masochistic practice rooted in hatred of one's body. The Church's understanding of fasting could not be more opposed to such a view. As part of the Christian life and an aid to prayer, fasting is a way to "acquire mastery over our instincts," as the *Catechism* teaches (*CCC* 2043). In other words, fasting is not about punishing our bodies, but rather understanding them rightly: it helps us to set our sights on heaven by teaching us to decrease our attachment to the things of earth.

WHY MIGHT A PERSON PRAY THIS WAY?

Pilgrimage

Making a pilgrimage to a shrine or holy site is a way of acknowledging God's action at a particular place and in a particular time, on behalf of a particular person or people. It is also a beautiful symbol of conversion: we leave our home and its comforts behind to venture into unfamiliar territory and journey toward God, trusting that God will provide for our material and spiritual needs and show us the way to draw closer to him in prayer. For people who feel that they have reached a plateau in their spiritual life and find themselves unsure of how to proceed, a pilgrimage can be an experience of spiritual intensity that can renew and reinvigorate one's commitment to building a stronger relationship with God.

In the wake of a traumatic life event, people sometimes feel that they need a change of scenery in order to obtain a clearer spiritual perspective; however, making a pilgrimage in such a situation may not be advisable. If you are considering a pilgrimage, talk it over with a trusted friend, spiritual companion, or spiritual director, and of course, bring the matter to God in prayer. Making a pilgrimage can be a powerful experience, but like fasting, it must be done for the right reasons. By journeying to a place where people of faith have experienced God's presence for generations, we express our faith that God is always present and at work in the world, our hope that he is present and at work in our own lives as well, and our love for and acceptance of the path he has laid before us to lead us back to himself.

Fasting

In Christian life today, fasting is encouraged as a way of preparing one's heart for a deeper encounter with the Lord: the Church practices fasting, along with prayer and almsgiving, during Lent to prepare for the celebration of Easter. Yet fasting is also a symbol of repentance—an acknowledgment that we have sinned against God and that we need God's forgiveness. In addition, fasting can be a way of intensifying our prayer for a particular intention, as we see in the Old Testament account of David, who fasted during the sickness of his son (see 2 Samuel 12:15–18). Fasting can also simply be a way of reminding ourselves of our complete dependence on God. Whatever your reason for taking up a fast, do so humbly, thoughtfully, and above all, prayerfully.

WHEN AND WHERE CAN ONE PRACTICE THIS FORM OF PRAYER?

Pilgrimage

There are many possibilities for places where you can make a pilgrimage, depending on where you live and what the circumstances of your life may permit in terms of travel. There may be a shrine within driving distance, or you may choose to journey farther from home. As we will see below, you may also simply choose to move through your own surroundings with greater spiritual attentiveness. Remember that a pilgrimage is not a vacation; the point is not to incur exorbitant expenses by flying first-class or staying in a fancy hotel, but to make this journey of faith in simplicity and poverty of spirit. As for timing, it is worth noting that some places of pilgrimage offer retreats at various times of the year, particularly during the Lenten season. Or, if your chosen site is associated with a particular saint, there may be unique opportunities for prayer on or around that person's feast day. Whether you walk the Camino to Santiago de Compostela in Spain, drive through the Rocky Mountains to the shrine of Mother Cabrini in Colorado, or light a candle at the replica of the Lourdes Grotto at the University of Notre Dame (or at a Marian shrine in your home diocese), your pilgrimage can provide an opportunity for prayer and reflection that may bear fruit in your relationship with God and others for the rest of your life.

Fasting

As noted above, although fasting is a practice typically associated with Lent, it can be done nearly anytime, in practically any place (depending on the kind of fast chosen). Traditionally, Fridays and Wednesdays have been observed as days for fasting. However, there are certain days in the liturgical year that are great celebrations, and these call for *feasting*, not fasting. Christmas and its twelve-day season, Easter and its eight-day octave, and solemnities such as the Annunciation (March 25) or the feast of St. Joseph (March 19) are times when the Church rejoices at the saving action of God in Christ. Fasting on such days would be incongruent with their festive nature.

HOW DOES ONE PRAY THIS WAY IN PRACTICE?

Pilgrimage

Traveling to Rome or the Holy Land on pilgrimage is a once-in-a-lifetime opportunity for some; for others, it may never be possible. Yet, because this is ultimately a spiritual practice, the geographical considerations are not the most important component: even if you lack the time or means to travel, you can still make a pilgrimage. Each Holy Thursday, many Christians make a pilgrimage in their own dioceses by participating in the tradition of visiting seven churches. These visits are made after the Evening Mass of the Lord's Supper ends, when the Eucharist has been moved to a special altar. The faithful are invited to keep watch in prayer with Jesus in anticipation of recalling his Passion and Death on Good Friday, and the movement from church to church recalls Jesus' movement from the upper room to the Garden of Gethsemane to his trial.

A prayer path or labyrinth is another way of using movement to make a spiritual pilgrimage. Some parishes, dioceses, and religious communities have created prayer paths lined with images of the Stations of the Cross or the Mysteries of the Rosary; others have constructed labyrinths on the grounds of their facilities. A labyrinth is usually a winding path laid out in a circular pattern that makes its way toward a center point. It symbolizes the journey inward toward God, who dwells in the hearts of his children. If the idea of praying with a labyrinth appeals to you, consider creating one in your backyard using simple stepping stones. You can make a spiritual pilgrimage without leaving your home.

Forms of processional prayer celebrated in parish communities are also a kind of pilgrimage. Parishes or dioceses dedicated to the patronage of Mary, Joseph, or one of the saints may hold great festivals on their feast days, carrying statues through the streets accompanied by prayer and singing, then celebrating long into the night with food and dancing. Find out if your parish hosts a eucharistic procession on the feast of Corpus Christi or celebrates *Las Posadas* during Advent. Not only are these processional forms of devotional prayer rich and beautiful pilgrimage experiences in themselves, but they are also wonderful ways to meet people in your parish community.

Fasting

The first step in fasting is setting the parameters. Examine your habits around food, drink, sleep, media, technology, or leisure, and decide what you will give up and for how long. If you are new to fasting, it's best to set reasonable limits that can be intensified as you grow accustomed to the practice. Start simply and start small; the habit of self-denial is one that must be built up gradually. While you should choose something that constitutes a genuine sacrifice, you will be more likely to persevere if you avoid taking on too much too soon. Keep in mind the obligations placed upon you by your personal and professional relationships: if your fasting is a burden for others, it will not help you or the people in your life grow closer to God. In addition, be mindful of any legitimate physical or spiritual limitations or obstacles that would rule out certain forms of fasting for you. Speak with your physician, therapist, spiritual director, or other trusted counselor before you begin a fast. Most importantly, be sure to incorporate prayer into your fast. Otherwise, you will miss the spiritual benefits that fasting offers. Name or write down the intention for which you are offering your fast, and choose a brief prayer for when you find yourself tempted to break it. Should you deliberately give in to this temptation or accidentally break your fast, don't give up, don't lose heart, and certainly don't punish yourself. Simply offer a prayer asking God to strengthen your resolve, and begin again.

Finally, to provide a healthy balance to your fasting, be sure to take the opportunities to rejoice with the Church by celebrating feast days throughout the liturgical year. Feasting in the Christian life does not mean overindulging or giving in to gluttonous behavior; rather, it helps us to celebrate the marvelous work of redemption that God has accomplished in Christ and to anticipate the unending joy of heaven.

8.

PRAYING WITH A
SACRED WORD

Be still and know that I am God!

—Psalm 46:11

WHAT IS THIS FORM OF PRAYER?

Several forms of prayer in the Christian tradition are rooted in the repetition of what is often referred to as a sacred word or a sacred phrase. On the surface, this practice can seem to be at odds with Jesus' teaching recorded in Matthew's Gospel: "In praying, do not babble like the pagans, who think that they will be heard because of their many words" (Matthew 6:7). However, in this instruction, Jesus is warning against a purely *quantitative* approach to prayer, in which one simply tries to rack up as many recitations and repetitions as possible, without giving any thought to what one is praying. Such prayer would certainly be considered babble! What is fascinating is that Jesus follows up this admonition against repetitive prayer by teaching his disciples the Our Father, or Lord's Prayer, which has been repeated countless times by countless Christians across the centuries. The fact that Jesus gives his disciples for all generations the gift of the Lord's Prayer indicates clearly that it is not the *act* of repeating one's prayers that presents a problem—he prefaces the Lord's Prayer by stating unequivocally, "This is how you are to pray" (Matthew 6:9). Rather, it is the *spirit* in which those prayers are offered—or rather, the *lack of spirit*—that makes a problem of repetitive prayer. When practiced with thought and care and attentiveness to the *quality* rather than the *quantity* of the repetitions, this form of prayer can be a powerful way of drawing close and staying close to God throughout the day, in whatever circumstances we may find ourselves.

Several different kinds of prayer in the Christian tradition incorporate repetition. Some familiar prayers such as the Rosary are composed of variety within repetition: the repeated prayers remain consistent throughout, but the mysteries that guide one's meditation change, inviting one to focus on different moments in the lives of Jesus and Mary. Litanies also fall into this category, combining a plethora of invocations with a few simple repeated responses. The consistency of the responses allows a greater depth of meditation on the beauty of the invocations, which are often a feast of scriptural and poetic imagery. Other prayers, such as the Divine Mercy Chaplet, are only varied insofar as there are several prayers that alternate with one another.

The two forms of prayer discussed in this chapter—the Jesus Prayer and its corollaries and centering prayer—most often involve repetition *without* variety, but they differ from each other in their manner of repetition. As a result, they also differ slightly in the particular purpose their repetitions serve. Nevertheless, the overarching goal of both prayers is the same: to quiet the chaotic mind and allow one to descend into the heart, where an encounter with God may take place.

The Jesus Prayer

The Jesus Prayer developed in Eastern communities of the early Christian Church; by the fourth century, it had already become an established practice beloved and encouraged by many saints. There are different versions of the Jesus Prayer, including "Lord Jesus, Son of God, have mercy on me, a sinner," or "Lord Jesus Christ, Son of the living God, have mercy on me, a sinner," or "Lord Jesus, have mercy on me." At the heart of all of them is the name of Jesus and a plea for mercy—the short phrase "Jesus, mercy" is yet another form. In fact, simply breathing forth the name "Jesus" is itself a version of the Jesus Prayer—perhaps the most profound version, for "Jesus" is not just a name. It is *the* name: "the name that is above every name" (Philippians 2:9), the only name by which we are saved (see Acts 4:12). As the *Catechism* teaches, "The name 'Jesus' contains all: God and man and the whole economy of creation and salvation. To pray 'Jesus' is to invoke him and to call him within us. His name is the only one that contains the presence it signifies" (*CCC* 2666). When we pray the name "Jesus," or any version of the Jesus Prayer, we are not performing some magic trick, summoning Jesus into our hearts. Jesus is already there. *He is always there*. Rather, the Jesus Prayer makes us *aware* of his presence and places us within Jesus as we acknowledge that he is ever within us.

Centering Prayer

Centering prayer is a form of Christian meditative prayer aimed at cultivating the interior silence necessary for a contemplative encounter with God. According to Fr. Thomas Keating, O.C.S.O., who wrote and taught about this practice of prayer for more than two decades, in centering prayer, we simply practice consenting to God's presence and action within us through the gentle repetition of a sacred word. As noted with the Jesus Prayer, God is always present within us, always desiring to act within us to draw us closer to himself, but we are not always aware of or open to this presence and this action. Centering prayer, in a sense, brings us home to ourselves by helping us make room for God within the dwelling place of our hearts.

It is important to remember that Christian meditation is distinct from other forms of meditation. First and foremost, as its name affirms, centering prayer is *prayer*. It is an *encounter* between the one praying and God. Unlike yoga or other forms of meditation, centering prayer is *not* a technique to be mastered, because mastering a technique is essentially a quest for control. The goal of technical mastery promises that, with enough work, one can consistently bring about the outcome one desires. Such an approach has no place in the life of prayer, where we are in fact called to *surrender* our desires for control and humbly open ourselves up to being changed by our encounter and relationship with God. To approach prayer as though it were a technique to be mastered makes the fatal mistake of placing prayer's orientation with us, which completely disregards the fundamental reality that prayer is a gift from God—that it is our response to God's invitation to be in relationship with him. Approaching prayer as a technique to be mastered ultimately renders authentic prayer impossible because it is centered on the self. Authentic prayer can only take place when one gazes on God in self-emptying love. By constantly placing practitioners in a posture of openness and humble surrender, centering prayer and other forms of Christian meditative prayer nurture awareness of prayer as God's gift and render one more and more capable of receiving that gift.

WHY MIGHT A PERSON PRAY THIS WAY?

Repetition in the tradition of Christian prayer serves an exceptionally beautiful purpose. It is like ascending a spiral staircase: one may seem to be going around in circles, but with each repetition, one is actually moving higher and higher. Praying the same words over and over calms the noise of the mind and allows us to access the depths of the heart, where we can focus not on the *what* of the prayer's words, but on the *Who* of our prayer: the One whom we meet when we pray, the One who has called us into relationship with himself and by whose gift of grace we pray in the first place. The silent or audible repetition of vocal prayers (prayers made up of words) can help to create an interior space for deep meditation upon divine mysteries or a contemplative encounter with God that goes beyond words or images. In its humble simplicity and its poverty of spirit, repetitive prayer is a gateway to a deep relationship with God. It is a prayer that can be practiced by *everyone*, no matter where you are in your journey of faith.

The Jesus Prayer

The Jesus Prayer is a simple and powerful way to "persevere in prayer" (Romans 12:12). When we pray it consistently, from the midst of our circumstances, we are inviting Jesus into our lives just as they are, not as we would have them be, and we are inviting him to transfigure the way we see our lives by conforming our vision to his own. Prayed with a spirit of openness and love, the Jesus Prayer can reorient our gaze, helping us to turn from ourselves to Christ, from the trials and temptations of earth to the promises of heaven.

Centering Prayer

Centering prayer offers an antidote to the epidemic of noise that characterizes life in contemporary society by teaching us to seek and embrace interior silence. So many people today are terrified of silence. They are unable to be alone in a quiet room for any extended period of time, preferring instead to extend themselves through technology to a world of endless entertainment and immediate gratification. Yet it is only in the space of silence that we are able to come to a better understanding of who we are, for it is only in silence that we are able to hear the voice of God, our Creator and Source of our being. God reveals himself, and reveals us to ourselves, in silence. Perhaps we shy away from the possibility of this revelation because we are afraid of what we will find, afraid that we will be asked to change. Perhaps we avoid silence because we are afraid of God and of ourselves. God calls us to move beyond our fear. God calls us to trust in his love for us. Over and over, we hear Jesus say to us in scripture, "Do not be afraid." In the practice of centering prayer, we gradually learn to surrender to the God who created and redeemed us out of love and who, out of love, calls us into relationship with himself. In so doing, we learn to respond to the One who "first loved us" (1 John 4:19) with a love that "drives out fear" (1 John 4:18), and we grow in our ability to be at home in ourselves and in God.

WHEN AND WHERE CAN ONE PRACTICE THIS FORM OF PRAYER?

The Jesus Prayer

The Jesus Prayer is actually *intended* to be prayed anywhere, anytime. There is a remarkable freedom in knowing that we are able to call upon the name of Jesus at any and every moment in our lives and that we are invited and encouraged to do so by Jesus himself: "If you ask anything of me in my name, I will do it" (John 14:14). What we ask in invoking the name of Jesus is nothing less than the presence of Jesus himself, a presence that is always and forever one of infinite love and mercy, a presence from which we can draw strength to face whatever confronts us. And, by his own promise, we know that Jesus will always answer our prayer, helping us grow in our awareness of his constant presence in our hearts with every prayerful repetition of his name.

Centering Prayer

Due to its nature, centering prayer is best practiced consistently at a specific, intentionally chosen time. Fr. Keating himself recommends the early morning, affirming that it is often easier to cultivate interior silence when one is emerging from the silence of sleep, before the noise and concerns of the day make their presence felt in the mind and heart. Keating also advises setting aside twenty to thirty minutes for centering prayer, with the possibility for extending that time occasionally once you are more practiced in it, but with the caution that one should not spend hours each day in centering prayer unless instructed to do so by a spiritual director. It is also best to engage in centering prayer in the same space—one that is as free as possible from literal clutter, as well as figurative clutter such as noise or other intrusive distractions. Remember that no physical space will ever be perfectly free of distractions, and even if you manage to create such a space, your own mind will still supply plenty of distractions. However, if you are able to persevere in centering prayer, over time, you will likely find that you notice the distractions less and less. Choose a time when you are mentally alert, and create a space where you can be physically rooted and comfortably still for the entirety of your time in centering prayer.

HOW DOES ONE PRAY THIS WAY IN PRACTICE?

The Jesus Prayer

Offering the Jesus Prayer doesn't have to be any more complicated than simply thinking the name "Jesus" or speaking it aloud in a spirit of receptivity to encountering God in Christ. Still, there are other elements that you can consider incorporating into this practice if you wish. The most basic of these is simply aligning your prayer with your breath. If you find yourself in a stressful situation, for example, inhale deeply and pray the name "Jesus" as you exhale. Take several deep breaths this way, asking Jesus to help you grow in your awareness of his presence within you. If you are praying a longer form of the Jesus Prayer, you can divide the words on the inhalation—"Lord Jesus Christ, Son of the living God"—and the exhalation—"have mercy on me, a sinner." Far from being a superficial or superstitious practice, aligning prayer with breath can serve as a powerful reminder of the fact that, for the Christian, "faith without prayer is impossible—as life is impossible without breath."[1]

In addition to the Jesus Prayer, many other short prayers can be offered in this way. "Abba, Father," and "Come, Holy Spirit," are also powerful invocations and can help us come to a greater awareness of and openness to the presence and activity of the triune God within us—Father, Son, and Holy Spirit. Verses from scripture have also been prayed in this repetitive, respirational fashion throughout Christian history, including "God, come to my assistance; Lord, make haste to help me," which is drawn from Psalm 70:2 and now forms the introduction to the Liturgy of the Hours. The first part of the prayer could be prayed on the inhale, the second part on the exhale. Other possibilities include: "My Lord and my God!" (John 20:28), "Into your hands, Lord, I commend my spirit" (see

Psalm 31:6; also Luke 23:46), or "Lord God, be my refuge and my strength" (see Psalm 46:2). If there are verses from scripture that particularly resonate with you, repeating them prayerfully according to the needs and circumstances that arise throughout each day over the course of your life is a simple yet beautiful way to etch the Word of God more and more deeply into your heart.

Centering Prayer

With regard to the actual practice of centering prayer, the particulars around time and space named above should first be considered carefully. Once these parameters have been determined, one must then think about and choose a sacred word that will provide a touchstone for centering prayer. According to Fr. Keating, the sacred word is a symbol of one's intentions: by returning to it throughout prayer when thoughts or distractions arise, it symbolizes the renewal of one's consent to the interior presence and action of God. With this in mind, the sacred word one chooses should not be something that evokes an emotional response, as this may ultimately be distracting because one may be tempted to focus on the emotion evoked by the prayer instead of the prayer itself. Rather, the sacred word should be one that indicates one's intent to enter into this time with God. Words of one or two syllables are best, and possibilities include: Jesus, Abba, Spirit, love, mercy, peace, open, trust, patience, grace, and so on.

Before entering into prayer, set an alarm to alert you when your time of prayer has ended, making sure to choose a gentle ring tone so that your prayer will conclude peacefully and not with a startled shock. Get into a posture that is comfortable, but not so comfortable that you will be in danger of falling asleep. Sit with your back straight and aligned. If you sit in a chair, place your feet flat on the floor; if you sit on the floor, cross your feet comfortably. Your hands can either be folded in a gesture of reverent focus or placed palms-up in your lap in a gesture of receptivity. When you have recollected yourself and are ready to begin, breathe deeply and close your eyes. This is a symbol of closing the door on your external world and entering your internal world, where God is waiting for you.

Gently and simply introduce your sacred word and allow yourself to just *be* in the presence of God who is within you. Centering prayer is a practice of *being*, not *doing*. Do not be anxious if thoughts arise—and they will arise. Do not grow angry with yourself if you are distracted—and you will be distracted. Simply accept that thoughts and distractions occur, let them pass you by without judging or engaging them, and return to your sacred word. Do this as many times as necessary. Over time, the noisiness in your mind will subside, and you will become better able to let go of your thoughts and emotions as you move deeper into interior silence. Remain in this interior silence as long as you are able, always returning gently to your sacred word when needed.

Once your alarm indicates that your chosen time for prayer has elapsed, do not rush to move on to the next task in your day. Just as you took time to recollect yourself before your prayer, take time to withdraw from your prayer as you conclude. Your breathing may have become more shallow during your time of centering prayer, so take this opportunity to inhale and exhale deeply and deliberately and move your body after spending time in stillness. As you make this transition, do not give in to the temptation to analyze the time you have just spent in prayer; what you may have experienced as a time of endless distractions or dryness may ultimately bear fruit in ways you could never imagine. Instead of second-guessing or asking yourself if you were "praying right," simply thank God for this time in his presence, perhaps by offering a Glory Be, and ask God to help you continue to be aware of his presence within you as you go forward from your time of prayer.

Centering prayer is not about exercising sheer willpower over ourselves; it is about surrendering our desire for control by cultivating an interior posture of radical openness and receptivity to God. It is ultimately a prayer of *patience*, where we wait in silence for God to speak. It is also a prayer of *perseverance*, for we cannot control when God will choose to speak to us, let alone what God will choose to say to us. As Keating says, "If you wait, God will manifest himself. Of course, you may have a long wait."[2] Through its use of a repeated sacred word, centering prayer combines elements of vocal and meditative prayer, and through its emphasis on cultivating an openness to God in interior silence, it can serve as an aid or even a gateway to contemplative prayer with the living God in a gaze of adoration and love.

9.

PRAYING THROUGH SILENCE

As the Father loves me, so I also love you. Remain in my love.

—John 15:9

WHAT IS THIS FORM OF PRAYER?

Contemplation, or contemplative prayer, is prayer that is deeper than words or images. It is prayer that has been distilled down to the essence of pure encounter with the living God. It is the simple prayer of the pure of heart, the prayer of resting, abiding, remaining in God's love. Contemplative prayer is the silent language of love, in the way that a husband and wife who have been together for many years can simply be in each other's presence without speaking, while still sharing a deep level of connection. Above all, contemplative prayer is characterized by passivity on the part of the one who prays. It is a kind of dynamic passivity in which the soul simply stands ready to receive the gift of God's presence, waiting patiently for as long as God asks her to wait. In contemplative prayer, we pray confidently with the psalmist: "Surely, I wait for the LORD" (Psalm 40:2), and in God's own time, God answers this patient waiting, this dynamic passivity, and bestows the gift of contemplative prayer.

The contemplative says to God in imitation of Jesus, "Thy will be done" (see Matthew 26:39, Mark 14:36, and Luke 22:42), and then waits for God to act in his heart. The contemplative prays with the Virgin Mary, "*Fiat*, may it be done unto me according to your word" (see Luke 1:38), and then waits patiently for God in complete surrender to the divine will, as radically open to the possibility that God may *not* act as to the possibility that God may act, and as joyful to remain in darkness as to receive God's light. As Trappist monk Thomas Merton (1915–1968) wrote in his book *Contemplative Prayer*,

> Contemplative prayer is, in a way, simply the prefer-
> ence for the desert, for emptiness, for poverty. . . . The
> contemplative is one who would rather not know than
> know. Rather not enjoy than enjoy. Rather not have
> *proof* that God loves him. He accepts the love of God
> on faith, in defiance of all apparent evidence. . . . Only
> when we are able to "let go" of everything within us,
> all desire to see, to know, to taste and to experience the
> presence of God, do we truly become able to experience
> that presence with the overwhelming conviction and
> reality that revolutionize our entire inner life.[1]

There is no action, no formula, no technique by which we can bring about the encounter with God that takes place within contemplative prayer. On the other hand, there is no level of theological knowl-edge or spiritual ability that we must reach in order to "qualify" for contemplative prayer. It is not a form of prayer reserved for the elite few; it is pure gift. Still, we can open ourselves up to the possibility of the contemplative encounter and prepare ourselves to receive the gift of contemplative prayer should God choose to bestow it by faith-fully cultivating our relationship with him through such practices of prayer as those described in the previous chapters.

WHY MIGHT A PERSON PRAY THIS WAY?

Contemplative prayer is a gift to be greatly desired. The introduction noted that it is often described as the "highest" form of personal prayer, yet observed that misperceptions can arise from that superlative. Therefore, it may be more helpful to think about contemplative prayer not as reaching the heights of holiness, but as plumbing the depths of intimacy with God. In her masterpiece *The Interior Castle*, St. Teresa of Ávila describes the contemplative encounter as one that takes place within "the innermost chamber [of the heart], where God dwells inside our souls."[2] It is the encounter of the Song of Songs:

> On my bed at night I sought him
> whom my heart loves—
> I sought him but I did not find him.
> "Let me rise then and go about the city,
> through the streets and squares;
> Let me seek him whom my soul loves."
> I sought him but I did not find him.
> The watchmen found me,
> as they made their rounds in the city:
> "Him whom my soul loves—have you seen him?"
> Hardly had I left them
> when I found him whom my soul loves.
> I held him and would not let him go
> until I had brought him to my mother's house,
> to the chamber of her who conceived me.
>
> —Song of Songs 3:1–4

Contemplative prayer is the encounter of deepest intimacy between the soul and her Beloved, the soul and her Bridegroom. It is the simple gaze of love between the soul and God; it is an encounter that increases the soul's thirst for God even as God's presence slakes it. The contemplative encounter expands the capaciousness of the soul and renders it more capable of loving as God loves. It is the desire for this kind of expansion of soul that we perceive in St. Augustine's plea to God: "The house of my soul is too small for you to enter: make it more spacious by your coming."[3]

WHEN AND WHERE CAN ONE PRACTICE THIS FORM OF PRAYER?

Although contemplative prayer itself is a distinct form of experiential encounter with God, our *entire* life of prayer can become suffused with the character of contemplation, thus orienting and capacitating us to receive God's gift of contemplative prayer. Contemplative prayer, at its heart, is characterized by pure openness to God and total emptiness of self. This openness is like that of an aperture in a camera lens that lets in more and more light as it is widened. The light itself does not change, but the aperture is able to receive more of it. However, the self-emptiness intended here is *not* one of self-negation, as is the goal in some forms of meditation. Rather, as with the dynamic passivity of contemplative prayer, this is an emptiness waiting to be filled. In the words of Caryll Houselander:

> It is not a formless emptiness, a void without meaning;
>   on the contrary it has a shape, a form given to it
>   by the purpose for which it is intended.
>
> It is emptiness like the hollow in the reed, the narrow
>   riftless emptiness, which can have only one destiny:
>   to receive the piper's breath and to utter the song
>   that is in his heart.
>
> It is emptiness like the hollow in the cup, shaped to
>   receive water or wine.

> It is emptiness like that of the bird's nest, built in a
> round warm ring to receive the little bird.[4]

We can cultivate this spirit of openness and emptiness whenever and wherever we pray by constantly striving to set aside our own agenda and ego. Of course, this does not mean that we should never come to God with our needs or intentions in our life of prayer. On the contrary, we should never hesitate to bring even the seemingly smallest concern to our loving God. However, cultivating openness and emptiness before God *does* mean praying with a spirit of detachment: we place our needs and our desires before God, but we must not grasp onto them or attempt to somehow control the outcome of our prayer (as though that were even possible). Instead, having made our petitions known, we must simply leave them at God's feet and humbly ask God to act in whatever way he sees fit, and then bless and thank God however he chooses to answer our prayers. Whenever and wherever we enter into prayer, cultivating this spirit of openness and emptiness will imbue whatever form of prayer we choose to practice with a *contemplative orientation.*[5]

HOW DOES ONE PRAY THIS WAY IN PRACTICE?

Again, the contemplative encounter with God is not something we ourselves can bring about in our prayer life. All we can do is open ourselves up to it by faithfully practicing the other forms of both vocal and meditative prayer. By cultivating the relationship with God in these other ways, the heart gradually becomes disposed and prepared to receive God's gift of contemplative prayer. As Merton explains,

> One cannot go beyond what one has not yet attained,
> and normally the realization that God is "beyond imag-
> es, symbols, and ideas" dawns only on one who has
> previously made a good use of all these things, . . . and
> having reached the limit of symbol and idea goes on to
> a further stage in which he does without them, at least
> temporarily.[6]

Having sought to nourish our relationship with God through fidelity to our chosen practices of prayer, should God choose to grant
us the gift of contemplative prayer, the only thing left for us to do
is to surrender completely—to give ourselves over to the silence of
divine love, in which "the Father speaks to us his incarnate Word,
who suffered, died, and rose," and in which "the Spirit of adoption
enables us to share in the prayer of Jesus" (*CCC* 2717).

This does not mean, however, that once one has been granted
the gift of contemplative prayer, all other forms of prayer can be
abandoned. Far from it. If God does grant the gift of contemplative
prayer, one must never presume that it will be granted again, nor
must one attempt to re-create the conditions in which the contemplative encounter took place so as to bring it about again. This would
be like trying to manipulate God or force God's hand. One must
return again and again with joy to the forms of vocal and meditative
prayer that will continue to nourish one's relationship with God,
for, as Merton goes on to say, these other forms of prayer and aids
to prayer—including those that have been discussed throughout
this book—"still have their place in the everyday ordinary life of the
contemplative,"[7] and in the light of contemplative prayer, they will
shine forth with an even lovelier radiance. God's gift of contemplative prayer is such that it transfigures the way we see our lives. Our
"gaze of faith, fixed on Jesus," is returned by a divine gaze of love,
a gaze that "illumines the eyes of our heart and teaches us to see

everything in the light of [Christ's] truth and his compassion for all [people]" (*CCC* 2715). This simple and direct experience of God's presence that is contemplative prayer encompasses and integrates our deepest selves, orienting the heart ever more deeply toward God, so that one's entire life is suffused with the light of divine love. As we shall see in our final chapter, this light of the love of God is then radiated out into the world when we manifest our life of prayer in a life of service to God and neighbor.

10.

PRAYING THROUGH ACTION

For just as a body without a spirit is dead, so also faith without works is dead.

—James 2:26

WHAT IS THIS FORM OF PRAYER?

The *Catechism* teaches that "prayer and *Christian life* are *inseparable*" (*CCC* 2745). The goal of all prayer is to transform the Christian into a more faithful icon of Jesus Christ, who said to his disciples on the night before he died, "I give you a new commandment: love one another. As I have loved you, so you also should love one another" (John 13:34). Later in that same conversation, Jesus explicitly names what this love must look like: "No one has greater love than this, to lay down one's life for one's friends" (John 15:13). It is through the life of prayer that we cultivate our love for God, but it is also through the life of prayer that God shows us how to express our love for him in turn by the love we show our neighbor.

In Luke's Gospel, Jesus offered a concrete image of such love in the parable of the good Samaritan, where the neighbor is identified as the one who did not hesitate to extend compassion, even to a man who viewed him as an enemy (see Luke 10:29–37). In Matthew's

Gospel, Jesus' parable of the last judgment demonstrates in inescapably vivid imagery precisely what actions this life of charity toward our neighbor includes (see Matthew 25:31–46). The sheep—those who are judged as righteous and deserving of eternal life—are those who served Christ himself by serving the least of his brothers and sisters: "For I was hungry and you gave me food, I was thirsty and you gave me drink, a stranger and you welcomed me, naked and you clothed me, ill and you cared for me, in prison and you visited me" (Matthew 25:35–36). In other words, the righteous are those who meet the needs of their brothers and sisters. The unrighteous are those who ignore them. The unrighteous are like the priest and the Levite in the parable of the good Samaritan: they were so focused on themselves, and may have even thought that they were fulfilling God's will by observing the laws of ritual purity, that they missed the opportunity to minister to God himself by serving him in the half-dead man on the side of the road. If we *only* focus on cultivating our own relationship with God through prayer to the exclusion of cultivating our relationship with our neighbor through service, then something is out of balance, and we must ask God to show us how to grow in our love for him *and* our love for our neighbor.

In the Christian tradition, the Corporal Works of Mercy are concrete practices by which we might show our love for God through our love of neighbor. Several of these practices, in fact, are drawn from the parable of the last judgment in Matthew's Gospel mentioned above; thus, they are practices identified by Jesus himself as ways of serving him by serving others.

1. Feed the hungry.
2. Give drink to the thirsty.
3. Clothe the naked.
4. Visit the imprisoned.
5. Shelter the homeless.

6. Visit the sick.
7. Bury the dead.

In addition, there are seven Spiritual Works of Mercy that we are also invited to practice in our Christian life. St. (Mother) Teresa of Calcutta (1910–1997) used to speak of Americans in particular as those who, despite their material wealth, suffered from great spiritual poverty. In practicing the Spiritual Works of Mercy, we can help others draw closer to God in Christ by humbly showing them Christ's love for them.

1. Instruct the ignorant.
2. Counsel the doubtful.
3. Comfort the sorrowful.
4. Admonish the sinner.
5. Bear wrongs patiently.
6. Forgive injuries.
7. Pray for the living and the dead.

WHY MIGHT A PERSON PRAY THIS WAY?

The life of charity, offered for love of one's neighbor—friends and enemies alike—out of love for God, is not only the fullest expression of the life of prayer, but it is also the extension of prayer into every moment of daily life. As Origen (d. 254) taught, "He 'prays without ceasing' [see 1 Thessalonians 5:17] who unites prayer to works and good works to prayer. Only in this way can we consider as realizable the principle of prayer without ceasing" (*CCC* 2745).[1] In addition, St. Thérèse of Lisieux (1873–1897) affirmed in her spiritual autobiography *Story of a Soul*, "The most beautiful thoughts are nothing without good works."[2] The same is true for the most beautiful prayers: they are nothing if they do not lead to good works.

Pope Benedict XVI takes this teaching a step further. Writing on liturgical prayer, he taught that "a Eucharist which does not pass over into the concrete practice of love is intrinsically fragmented."[3] If our participation in the Mass does not transform how we live our lives throughout the rest of the week, we have failed to receive fully the graces Jesus offers us in his eucharistic gift of self. The same thing can be said of personal prayer: it does not matter if we spend hours upon hours in private, intense prayer each day. Prayer that never "[passes] over into the concrete practice of love" for our brothers and sisters is "intrinsically fragmented" because it is ultimately self-centered—thus, in the end, it is not authentic prayer at all. As St. John wrote in his first epistle, "If anyone says, 'I love God,' but hates his brother, he is a liar" (1 John 4:20a). It is equally true that if anyone says, "I love God," but *ignores the needs of* his brother or sister, he is a liar. St. John continues, "For whoever does not love a brother whom he has seen cannot love God whom he has not seen. This is the commandment we have from him: whoever loves God must also love his brother" (1 John 4:20b–21).

All of the various forms of prayer discussed in this book are not meant to be practiced as a way of drawing closer *exclusively* to God in faith; they must be understood as means of drawing closer to our neighbor in charity as well. No Christian is a disciple unto himself or herself; we belong to Christ *and* to one another by virtue of the fact that we are all members of Christ's Body (see Romans 14:7–8). Not only that, but we are called to extend our charity even to those who are not Christians, for Christ came to redeem the entire human family, and we are called to share this Good News with everyone whom we encounter. Indeed, Jesus identifies this life of charity as the very thing that will draw others in and open them up to him and his teachings: "This is how all will know that you are my disciples, if you have love for one another" (John 13:35). It is the Christian love of neighbor, offered for love of God, that paves the way for evangelization. It is love that builds up the kingdom of God on earth. It is love that integrates prayer with action—love of God with love of neighbor—such that the entire life of the one who loves becomes a prayer offered to God.

WHEN AND WHERE CAN ONE PRACTICE THIS FORM OF PRAYER?

Prayer and the Christian life are indeed inseparable, and the life of prayer does indeed bear fruit in the life of charity, but this does not mean that we can simply substitute one for the other. We must still set aside specific times for each. We will never be able to "pray without ceasing" in a life of charity unless we set aside time each day when we are devoted to prayer and nothing else. St. Teresa of Calcutta provides a truly marvelous example of this integrated approach to prayer and service. Known throughout the world for her total gift of self in service to the poorest of the poor, she insisted over and over that it was only by spending hours each day in prayer before the Blessed Sacrament that she and her sisters, the Missionaries of Charity, were able to minister to others. She understood better than most people that time devoted exclusively to prayer is time when the branches draw the most nourishment from the True Vine. Contemplation and action are two sides of the same coin: contemplation is expressed in action, and action is nourished by contemplation. In other words, the life of prayer is the fuel that feeds the life of charity. We cannot have one without the other.

HOW DOES ONE PRAY THIS WAY IN PRACTICE?

Looking at the lists of the Corporal and Spiritual Works of Mercy can be intimidating. You may not know where to begin. But remember that no action is small when offered in great love. Jesus taught that even someone who offers a little one a cold cup of water out of love for him will be rewarded in heaven (see Matthew 10:42). Remember, too, the approach that the righteous embodied in the parable of the last judgment: they did not have a list of tasks that they checked off every day; they simply practiced mercy whenever and wherever they could, within the context of their lives. The Works of Mercy are not to-do lists. As Pope Francis indicated, they are guides for a Christian way of life:

> The Christian life involves the practice of the traditional seven corporal and seven spiritual works of mercy. We usually think of the works of mercy individually and in relation to a specific initiative: hospitals for the sick, soup kitchens for the hungry, shelters for the homeless, schools for those to be educated, the confessional and spiritual direction for those needing counsel and forgiveness. . . . But if we look at the works of mercy as a whole, we see that *the object of mercy is human life itself and everything it embraces*.[4]

With that in mind, the place to begin when thinking about how to practice mercy is your own life, precisely as it is right now. Think about your relationships with other people: your spouse or significant other, your children, your parents or siblings, your colleagues and friends. If you are a parent caring for an infant or young child, or if you are an adult caring for an aging or ill parent, you likely won't be able to volunteer at a local soup kitchen for three hours every night, but you can practice mercy every time you change a diaper, pick up medicine from the pharmacy, or sit by a sickbed in the middle of the night.

As you practice these hidden works of mercy in the context of your daily life, try to root them intentionally in your life of prayer as well. If you find yourself struggling to respond to your children's needs with patience and kindness, make an act of offering in the midst of the situation: take a second to breathe deeply and say a silent prayer, such as, "All for you, Lord Jesus," or "To Jesus through Mary," or "Help me to love you in my children, Jesus" (or "in my spouse," or "in my mother," or "in my boss," whatever the situation calls for). Consistently practicing small works of mercy can be incredibly challenging; placing them within the context of prayer can help to reframe the situation and remind you of the One who is present in those whom you are serving, even if they themselves are being difficult.

While it is important to begin with your life as it is now in practicing the works of mercy, it is also important to eventually begin discerning opportunities for more traditional forms of service if this is not already a part of your life. If the circumstances of your life at the moment are truly such that committing to volunteer service is not possible, consider whether you might be able to support organizations committed to the poor through financial contributions until such time that you are able to support them in volunteering or other forms of service. In advocating for practices of mercy rooted in daily interactions and close relationships, Pope Francis was not excusing Christians from seeking out ways to serve the poor and the marginalized. Rather, for the one who has intentionally cultivated the practice of mercy in everyday life, it is a natural next step to go out into the world and serve Christ in the needy and vulnerable. The former can serve as a foundation for the latter, and the latter can serve as an affirmation of and inspiration for the former, resulting in an integrated, seamless approach to practicing mercy in ways both large and small. Whatever form these practices of mercy take, as long as their foundation is that of prayer, one can be confident that the love of neighbor will always be rooted in the love of God. Over time, prayer manifested in acts of mercy and acts of mercy nourished by prayer will mutually fan the flame of divine love within the heart, until one's whole life becomes a prayer offered to God in grateful praise.

NOTES

INTRODUCTION TO CHRISTIAN PRAYER

1. Augustine of Hippo, *The Confessions of Saint Augustine*, trans. John K. Ryan (New York: Doubleday, 1960), I, 1.

2. See Augustine, *Confessions*, III, 6, 11.

3. Citing Teresa of Ávila, *The Book of Her Life*, 8, 5, in *The Collected Works of St. Teresa of Ávila*, trans. K. Kavanaugh, O.C.D., and O. Rodriguez, O.C.D. (Washington, DC: Institute of Carmelite Studies, 1976), I, 67.

4. *G. K. Chesterton: Collected Works*, vol. 1 (San Francisco: Ignatius Press, 1986), 350.

5. Romano Guardini, *The Art of Praying: The Principles and Methods of Christian Prayer*, trans. Prince Leopold of Loewenstein-Wertheim (Manchester, NH: Sophia Institute Press, 1985), 7.

3. PRAYING THROUGHOUT THE DAY

1. This prayer is known as the Shema because its first word, "Hear," is *Shema* in Hebrew.

2. The *Didache* (which means "teaching") is a short treatise on the Christian life written in Greek. It is one of the oldest documents available that describes prayer practices of the first Christian communities.

3. Citing Thomas Aquinas, *Summa Theologica,* II-II, 83, 9.

4. At that time, the Hail Mary consisted only of what is now the first half of the prayer, which includes the "angelic

greeting"—Gabriel's words to the Blessed Mother (Luke 1:28)—and Elizabeth's benediction (Luke 1:42). The second part of the prayer ("Holy Mary, Mother of God . . .") consists of a prayer for intercession at the hour of death and was added to the *Ave Maria* by 1493.

5. A high-quality photo of *L'Angelus* can be viewed on the Musée d'Orsay's website, https://m.musee-orsay.fr/en/works/commentaire_id/the-angelus-339.html.

6. With the thrice-daily approach, the Angelus is traditionally prayed at 6:00 a.m., 12:00 p.m., and 6:00 p.m.

7. Traditionally, one either bows or genuflects on the phrase "And the Word became flesh" to honor the Incarnation—the moment the Son of God was conceived in Mary's womb—with one's own body.

4. PRAYING WITH SACRED SCRIPTURE

1. Lectio divina can include sacred texts other than scripture, such as those written by the saints over the centuries or those included in the Office of Readings in the Liturgy of the Hours. For someone just beginning lectio divina, however, it is highly recommended to focus on praying with scripture at first, as it is a privileged place of encountering God himself.

2. The daily readings for Mass are available at the website for the United States Conference of Catholic Bishops (usccb.org), or in monthly publications such as *Magnificat* or *Give Us This Day*. Each of these publications also contains adapted versions of Morning, Evening, and Night Prayer that can be used for lectio divina; however, these generally do not use the proper psalms and canticles from the Liturgy of the Hours, which can be found at multiple websites (e.g., universalis.com).

5. PRAYING THROUGH EXPERIENCE

1. Timothy M. Gallagher, O.M.V., *The Examen Prayer: Ignatian Wisdom for Our Lives Today* (New York: Crossroad, 2006), 40.

2. For an outline of the Examen based on the *Spiritual Exercises*, see Gallagher, *The Examen Prayer,* 25.

3. *The Examen Prayer,* 75, citing the *Spiritual Exercises,* no. 43.

6. PRAYING THROUGH BEAUTY

1. *De sacris imaginibus orationes,* 1.27; cited in Timothy Verdon, *Art & Prayer: The Beauty of Turning to God* (Brewster, MA: Paraclete Press, 2014), vi.

2. Many high-quality photographs of Michelangelo's *Pietà* are available online. The Vatican website also offers a virtual tour that allows you to see the *Pietà* within St. Peter's Basilica, http://www.vatican.va/various/basiliche/san_pietro/vr_tour/Media/VR/St_Peter_Pieta/index.html.

3. While you can notice the beauty of a church if you are there for Mass, it's better to do so when the church is empty and quiet and you can let your eyes linger at a prayerful pace.

8. PRAYING WITH A SACRED WORD

1. Guardini, *The Art of Praying,* 8.

2. Thomas Keating, O.C.S.O., *Open Mind, Open Heart: The Contemplative Dimension of the Gospel,* 20th anniversary edition (London: Bloomsbury, 2006), 24.

9. PRAYING THROUGH SILENCE

1. Thomas Merton, *Contemplative Prayer* (New York: Image, 2014), 67.

2. Teresa of Ávila, *The Interior Castle*, trans. Mirabai Starr (New York: Riverhead Books, 2003), 280.

3. Augustine, *Confessions*, I, 5, 6.

4. Caryll Houselander, *The Reed of God* (Notre Dame, IN: Ave Maria Press, 2006), 21.

5. Merton, *Contemplative Prayer*, 92.

6. Merton, *Contemplative Prayer*, 63.

7. Merton, *Contemplative Prayer*, 63.

10. PRAYING THROUGH ACTION

1. Citing Origen, *De Oratione,* 12: PG 11, 452C.

2. Thérèse of Lisieux, *Story of a Soul*, Study Edition, trans. John Clarke, O.C.D., ed. Marc Foley, O.C.D. (Washington, DC: ICS Publications, 2019), 375.

3. Benedict XVI, *Deus Caritas Est* (2005), 14.

4. Francis, *Message for the Celebration of the World Day of Prayer for the Care of Creation* (2016), emphasis added.

Carolyn Pirtle is program director at the Notre Dame Center for Liturgy in the McGrath Institute for Church Life at the University of Notre Dame, where she also is the managing editor of and a frequent contributor to the McGrath Institute Blog. She earned her master's degrees in theology and sacred music at Notre Dame and a master's degree in music at Kansas State University, where she received a bachelor's degree in music.

Pirtle is an award-winning composer of liturgical and non-liturgical music and has been commissioned by organizations including the South Bend Chamber Singers, Saint Mary's College, and the University of Notre Dame. Her music has been published by World Library Publications and earthsongs.

Pirtle previously served as director of music and elementary music instructor at St. John Berchmans Parish in Chicago, Illinois. She also cofounded and served as the house director of the House of Brigid community in Ireland. Pirtle is the author of *Praying the Rosary Together*. She has been a guest on Redeemer Radio and Sacred Heart Radio.

She lives in South Bend, Indiana.

Facebook: Carolyn Pirtle
Twitter: @carolyn_pirtle

The McGrath Institute for Church Life was founded as the Center for Pastoral and Social Ministry by the late–Notre Dame president Fr. Theodore Hesburgh, C.S.C., in 1976. The McGrath Institute partners with Catholic dioceses, parishes, and schools to provide theological education and formation to address pressing pastoral problems. The Institute connects the Catholic intellectual life to the life of the Church to form faithful Catholic leaders for service to the Church and the world. The McGrath Institute strives to be the preeminent source of creative Catholic content and programming for the new evangelization.

www.mcgrath.nd.edu

MORE IN THE
ENGAGING CATHOLICISM
SERIES

A recent Pew study found that almost seventy percent of Catholics don't believe that Jesus is really present in the Eucharist. Rather, they see the bread and wine of Communion as mere symbols of Christ's body and blood, not the real thing— a central belief of the faith. Is it just a misunderstanding or a blatant rejection of the Church's teachings?

In *Real Presence*, University of Notre Dame theologian Timothy P. O'Malley clears up the confusion and shows you how to embrace Christ present in the Eucharist with your whole being.

"This book is essential reading at our moment in the Church's history."

—Mike Aquilina

Catholic author and executive vice president
of the St. Paul Center for Biblical Theology

Look for more titles in this series wherever books and eBooks are sold.

Visit avemariapress.com for more information.